the

the heart

vessantara

Windhorse Publications

Also by Vessantara
Meeting the Buddhas
Tales of Freedom
The Mandala of the Five Buddhas
The Vajra and Bell
Female Deities in Buddhism
The Five Female Buddhas
The Breath

Published by
Windhorse Publications Ltd
11 Park Road
Birmingham
B13 8AB
UK
email: info@windhorsepublications.com
web: www.windhorsepublications.com

Cover design: Satyadarshin
Printed by Cromwell Press Ltd, Trowbridge, England

British Library Cataloguing in Publication Data:
A catalogue record for this book is available from the British Library

ISBN-10: 1 899579 71 0
ISBN-13: 978 1 899579 71 6

contents

about the author

Vessantara was born in London in 1950. Interested in Buddhism since his teens, he first had direct contact with Buddhists in 1971. In 1974 he became a member of the Western Buddhist Order and was given his Buddhist name, which means 'universe within'. He has a particular interest in Tibetan Buddhism and has had several Tibetan teachers.

He holds an MA in English from Cambridge University and a professional social work qualification. He is the author of eight books, including *Meeting the Buddhas* and *Tales of Freedom*, and has led retreats and workshops in Europe, the USA, India, and Australasia.

He is currently based in Cambridge, England, and divides his time between periods of intensive meditation, writing, and teaching.

acknowledgements

Writing about loving-kindness meditation is itself a very heart-opening activity. While working on this book I have felt appreciative of many people.

I first practised the meditation described in this book in London in 1973, at a centre run by the Friends of the Western Buddhist Order. The teaching followed the approach of Sangharakshita, from whom I have gained a great deal over many years. More recently I have benefited greatly from my contact with Lama Shenpen Hookham, and her style of teaching based on Mahamudra and Dzogchen. My approach draws on both these teachers, but it shouldn't be taken as representing the thinking of either of them.

Since the late 1980s I have also gained immensely from my contact with Dagyab Kyabgön Rinpoche, an eminent Tibetan lama based in Germany. In writing about the heart, I have called him to mind again and again as an exemplar of kindness and open-heartedness.

the breath

These three people have been the primary influences on this book, but there have been many others, too numerous to remember, let alone acknowledge. These include helpful discussions with friends and colleagues who teach this meditation, as well as stimulation and questions from people I have taught over the years.

Maitrivajri and Vijayamala both read early drafts of this book and gave me very helpful feedback. I also benefited from reading part of an unpublished manuscript on loving-kindness meditation by Viveka, who chairs the San Francisco Buddhist Center. Bahiya kindly allowed me to borrow one of his stories.

My editor, Jnanasiddhi, and I have worked together on several books now. As ever, she has been perceptive about the text and supportive of its author. And for this book, which has not had an easy birth, she has also had to be patient and forgiving.

Each year the staff at Windhorse Publications is responsible for thousands of people learning more about meditation and Buddhism. In their unostentatious way they are working for a better world. I appreciate their dedication.

To all the above, I offer my heartfelt gratitude.

Vessantara
Cambridge
17 August 2006

introduction

*The best and most beautiful things in the world
cannot be seen or even touched,
they must be felt with the heart.*
Helen Keller

valuing the heart

Our heart, that deep place in which we respond to
'the best and most beautiful things in the world', is a
mystery that we sometimes take for granted. Yet our
heart responses are fundamental to every aspect of
ourselves. With our heart we decide what we want to
do with our lives, what we have 'our heart set on'.
Our heart is crucial to whether we are likely to suc-
ceed at anything; if our heart isn't in it, then we probably won't. Our heart even determines whether life is
worth living; if we're broken-hearted, we may want
to die. It has a lot to do with whether we think someone is a decent human being. Are they good-hearted,
or hard-hearted? And we know that we have really
communicated deeply with someone when we have a
heart-to-heart communication. Somehow our heart

feels like the centre of what we are as a person. It isn't coincidence that we talk about getting to the heart of something.

Although we use our rational faculty a great deal, when we want deeper knowledge it is to our heart that we turn. Although we can be led astray by affairs of the heart (which is a more superficial, romantic experience), we still experience what is finally true about ourselves in our heart of hearts. In fact, although we often seem to work on the basis that we are what we think, when we point to ourselves we always indicate our heart, never our head.

Although we use this language quite naturally, we might never have explored the experience that it is pointing at. What *does* lie at the heart of our experience? Who or what *are* we as human beings? We know that we feel better when we are open-hearted, but that seems to come and go. Is there any way of reliably bringing about that feeling? There are times when our heart goes out to many people – perhaps after some natural disaster. Is there any limit to that feeling? How many people can we hold in our heart?

Buddhism has been exploring these issues for 2,500 years. Over that time it has developed many methods to help us go deep into the mystery of the human heart and to find answers to these questions. The answers are not theoretical, generated by the rational mind, but direct knowledge, from our own experience. Buddhist meditation is essentially a way of helping us to explore our experience, and to respond creatively to what we find.

In this short book we shall learn some methods from the Buddhist tradition that will enable us to explore our own hearts, and to develop more satisfying ways of being. These methods can help us to become more loving and compassionate towards others, and kinder and more understanding towards ourselves.

If you look at your experience, you will notice that when you are being genuinely and freely kind and loving you also feel happier and more fulfilled. So learning and practising these meditation methods can also raise your general level of contentment and enjoyment of life.

Big claims? I'm certainly not suggesting that these methods are effortless or a quick fix. Meditation requires a gentle persevering effort, and a willingness not to deceive yourself. Given that basic level of commitment and integrity, you needn't be anyone special at all. You don't have to be particularly intelligent, or able to sit in the full lotus posture, or be a conventionally good person. The methods are all quite simple, and they will work for anyone who practises them reasonably sincerely. To help motivate you to give them a try, let's look at some of the benefits you can expect from the meditation.

benefits of the meditation
The main meditation we shall be learning helps develop friendliness, kindness, and love. It's a way of opening your heart, though not in a naive way, to people around you (and includes learning to be on good terms with yourself as well!). This meditation has been praised by Buddhist teachers down the

ages, starting with the Buddha himself in the *Metta Sutta*, or 'Discourse on Loving-Kindness'.[1] One traditional text[2] lists eleven different benefits of the regular practice of the meditation, including

Sleeping and waking in comfort

Not having bad dreams

Having other people treat you with warmth and affection

Being able to concentrate easily

Being serene

Dying in a clear state of mind

From my experience of teaching this meditation, and watching hundreds of people practise it regularly, I would flesh out the list with some other benefits. It can help you to be:

more deeply emotionally aware. Although people vary a lot in this regard, our experience of our emotions is often not very clear, like watching a black and white movie on an old TV with a fuzzy picture. Through this meditation we come to know our feelings much more deeply, in all their vivid colours. This is very satisfying. We often search for intimacy with another person when we have not come into much intimate contact with our own feelings. We also often have quite a limited emotional range. This meditation enables us to acknowledge the full spectrum of our feelings.

more open-hearted, kinder, and more loving. The meditation doesn't just make you aware of what you are feeling, it also gives you tools for working with your emotions so that gradually – over time, not overnight – you discover the store of love and care that we all carry around buried in our hearts.

more patient, and more able to handle frustration. This meditation is traditionally recommended as an antidote to anger and hatred. I know many people who have found it a valuable part of an anger management course. Greater emotional awareness enables you to catch difficult feelings earlier, and to break out of the tendency to bounce between denying feelings and then being carried away by them.

more emotionally buoyant. You can develop a reservoir of energy that enables you to throw off difficulties that in the past would have got you down.

more at ease with yourself. Many people are not on very good terms with themselves. This meditation enables you to be a friend to yourself and to see yourself much more sympathetically.

more spontaneous and engaged with life. The meditation frees up emotional blocks and re leases energy. As your emotions become more positive, you can trust that your first response in any situation is likely to be helpful and appropriate, so you don't have to keep yourself reined in for fear of saying or doing something that you might regret.

better able to relate to different kinds of people. The meditation gives you practice in empathizing with others. You become better at valuing and appreciating people who are very different from you.

more capable of responding positively to the suffering in the world, without feeling overwhelmed by it. Sometimes our hearts go out to people, but after a while we find we have nothing left to give. This meditation gives you greater emotional resources. It is particularly useful for people in the helping professions, who have to deal with suffering every day, and can sometimes fall into a cold, 'professional' detachment or become overly involved and emotionally exhausted.

These benefits all make the meditation very valuable in itself, but there is more. Buddhism has tremendous belief in what we can achieve as human beings. Its goal is a state of deep wisdom, in which we clearly see the true nature of our experience. From that enlightened perspective, we realize we are not ultimately separate from other living beings, and that we all create our own suffering, through basing our lives on misunderstandings about how things are. This wisdom then gives birth to a profound compassion, because we feel complete solidarity with suffering beings, and we know that their suffering is all, in a sense, unnecessary.

This state of wisdom and compassion doesn't appear out of nowhere. It is traditionally said to be the result of following a long path over many lifetimes. However, it is certainly possible within this life to gain glimpses of wisdom – direct intuitive understanding of life's true nature – and to unfold the compassion that goes with it. This experience, which represents a radical transformation of yourself as a human being, is known in Buddhism as the arising of the heart of awakening, or awakened heart.[3] The meditation that you will learn here can really open your heart, and set up excellent conditions for the arising of deep wisdom and compassion.

This may all sound a lot to take on, and you may simply want to learn the meditation in order to become kinder, more patient, or to have more emotional energy. That's fine. You don't have to bother with the advanced stages of the Buddhist path at all. But we all yearn for a truly fulfilling experience. Some of us are looking for it in churches or temples, others in shopping malls or clubs, but that is what we are all searching for as human beings. It's good to be aware that meditation can help you move in the direction of that experience.

how to use this book

I was brought up in a family who were very keen on sport, so when reading newspapers I always started from the back, a habit I carried over into my other reading. While this saved me a lot of time on whodunits, I wouldn't recommend it for a book like this. By all means read ahead, but the core of the book is the exercises and meditations it contains. These are designed to help you move step by step into a deeper relationship with your heart. So it would be best to work through them sequentially. You will not get the same benefit if you jump between them.

I introduce most of the exercises and meditations in chapters 1 to 3. Chapter 4 deals with preparing to enter and leave the meditation. If you have practised meditation before, you might want to skip this chapter, or skim it to see if there is anything new to you. Chapters 5 to 7 provide a range of useful ways of working with the meditation. It will be hard to get very far with it unless you use some of these methods. Most of the rest of the book explores issues that might come up in the meditation and suggests ways to understand how it works and how to take it deeper. Naturally, I wrote all this in the sequence I thought would be easiest and most helpful for the average reader. But if you're someone who likes to explore things in your own way, feel free to do some off-piste reading.

the heart and the breath

This is the second book in a series on the art of meditation. The first – *The Breath* – provided some basic groundwork in meditation, such as guidelines for sitting posture. This book doesn't cover that ground in the same detail, but it will give you enough information to enable you to begin and continue a meditation practice. In that respect, it stands alone, and you don't need to have read the first one. Even so, to widen your understanding of the basics, and to learn another meditation that complements what you will be learning here, it would be helpful to read *The Breath*.

If you are already practising meditation on the breath, I suggest you continue to do that, to maintain continuity, while you are reading the first few chapters of this book. If you want to use some of your meditation time to try out the exercises here, you could begin by meditating on the breath, but shorten the time you spend on it, and use the rest of the time to explore one of these exercises. Once you have learned the whole five-stage method of meditation taught here, you could alternate the two practices. So if you usually meditate once a day you could focus on the breath one day and on the heart the next.

working with a teacher

This book will give you a good introduction to 'heart-based' meditation. However, although you can set up a meditation practice by learning from a book like this, in the long run you will get further by practising with an experienced meditation teacher. I'll say a little more about this in the final chapter. There are different ways of teaching these meditations. If you have a teacher who suggests a slightly different method of practice then I suggest you follow their way of doing things. You can still read this book for further inspiration and helpful suggestions.

1

exploring your heart

> *Friends can help each other. A true friend is some-one who lets you have total freedom to be yourself – and especially to feel. Or not feel. Whatever you happen to be feeling at the moment is fine with them. That's what real love amounts to – letting a person be what he really is.*
> Jim Morrison

Although some people take to heart-based medita-tion like mallards to a mill pond, others find it hard to connect with. So rather than diving straight into it, we're going to approach it through some preliminary stages. Before you try to improve a situation, it is usu-ally helpful to get to know and understand it as it is. So before doing anything to change your emotional experience, you need to take a kindly interest in what is there already. This kindly interest in your present experience is itself the beginning of the process of opening your heart.

In this chapter I'm going to suggest four exercises for exploring aspects of your present experience. I've found them useful as a way of laying a good foundation for the meditation you will learn in the next couple of chapters. So feel free to repeat any or all of them as much as you like. In fact it would be good to do each of them a number of times, both to familiarize yourself with them and to become more aware of the way in which your physical and emotional experience changes from day to day.

We'll begin with an exercise that focuses on the body. This is a good preparation for meditation, as it helps to ground us in our present experience. (Our mind tends to flit around – diving into the future, searching back into the past, or spinning off into fantasies – but our physical sensations are always happening right here and now.) Also, all our feelings take place within the body. If we are joyful, angry, anxious, or full of love, all these emotions register in our posture, our breathing, in patterns of muscular tension and relaxation, and other physical effects. So becoming more aware of our body gives us all kinds of clues to what we are feeling, and indirect ways of working with our emotions.

exercise 1 – exploring physical sensations

Sit down in a comfortable posture, with your back straight, so that you feel relaxed but alert. If you have serious difficulty in sitting for any length of time, you can do the exercise lying down, but sitting is preferable as you are likely to be more awake. Most people will find it easier to do this exercise with their eyes closed. (These instructions apply to all the exercises in this book.) Now, not taking for granted that you know what it is like, but with a sense of curiosity, begin to explore your experience of your body. Can you feel your contact with the chair or cushion? Be aware of the solidity of that contact. With that feeling of the ground supporting you, you can relax and give your weight to the earth. Out of that sense of groundedness in your lower body, allow your spine to rise up naturally, not forcing it. (This exercise is a preliminary to developing loving-kindness, so you can start right here by being kind and gentle with yourself.)

Once you have a sense of a grounded but alert posture, spend a few minutes allowing your attention to roam through your physical sensations. If you want, you can do this systematically, working from the crown of your head down to the soles of your feet. (If you're feeling tired, it would be better to work the other way, from your feet upwards.) Or you can simply allow one sensation to lead you to the next, as different parts of your body attract your attention.

However you do it, let your awareness of your body be sympathetic. Try to leave your likes and dislikes to one side. Whatever you feel about it, your body is your life companion, faithfully accompanying you every step of your journey. It is the product of an amazing array of conditions, and is always doing its best for you in your particular circumstances. So allow your awareness of it to be as kind and appreciative as possible. This will itself have a positive, healing effect.

Then, when you feel the time is right, widen your awareness to include a sense of your surroundings, and open your eyes. Slowly move your body a little, and when you are ready, get up. (It is good to get into the habit of moving slowly and gently at the end of all med- itative exercises, even if you didn't feel very concentrated.)

In the second exercise we move on from experiencing the physical sensations of the body – heat, pressure, and so on – to exploring the pleasant and unpleasant feelings associated with them. As we are living beings, all our experience comes accompanied by a feeling tone, either pleasant, unpleasant, or neutral. The aim of this exercise is to develop your capacity to be aware of what is going on in this aspect of your experience. This is important because it is on the foundations of these simple pleasant and unpleasant feelings that our emotional life is built.

exercise 2 – experiencing feelings

Again begin by scanning through your body, making contact with the physical sensations as in the previous exercise. This helps to ground your awareness in the present moment. When you have done this for a few minutes, begin to scan through your body again, but this time noticing where your sensations are pleasant and enjoyable, unpleasant or uncomfortable, or just neutral. Again, do this in a non-judgemental way, with a kindly awareness. Just let things be. Don't try to change anything. Allow yourself to explore your experience as it is, taking a friendly interest in it. What sensations can you discover? When you feel the time is right, end the exercise as you did the previous one.

This attitude of being able to notice pleasant and un- pleasant feelings without reacting to them is a very useful one to develop. Life throws an ever-changing mixture of pleasure and pain at us. It is good to learn not to be led around by the nose by these feelings, but to be able to develop a spacious attitude in which we experience them but we don't allow them to take away our freedom.

In the next exercise we move from noticing pleasant and unpleasant feelings to exploring our emotions and moods.

exercise 3 – acknowledging moods and emotions

Once again sit quietly, close your eyes, and turn your attention to what is happening inside. This time, allow yourself to become aware of your emotional state, your current mood. When you start to identify it, stay with it, adopt a curious attitude to it, and see what you can learn about it. To help make it clearer, you can ask yourself questions, such as what would be the best description in words for what I'm feeling? Where in my body do I feel it? If it was a colour, what would that be? If it was a piece of music, what would it sound like? Notice any changes in it as a result of doing the exercise.

On different days, this exercise may strike you as very easy or quite hard. For instance, if someone has just upset or annoyed you, the feeling of upset or annoyance is likely to be very easy to find. Then it is just a question of being very curious about it. What is this experience that we call 'upset' or 'annoyance'? What is it really like? Your first response is often to 'bounce off' the feeling, thinking, 'It's obvious what it's like; the feeling is right in my face at the moment.' But there is always more to discover; a deeper experience is waiting for you if you keep alert and curious about what is going on.

It's important to understand that we're not interested here in the story that comes with the feeling, or the judging thoughts that tend to come with it. Someone might have treated you badly at work, which sets off the upset or annoyance, but during the exercise you don't focus on the work saga, replaying it in your mind and imagining what you could have said, or rehearsing what you'll do next time. You stay very clearly in the present moment, allowing yourself to experience the pure feeling, just as it is. You can think about how to solve your work difficulty at another time.

Although your feelings might sometimes be very strong when you do this exercise, at other times you might find you can't identify your feelings very clearly at all. It may be that you have not previously paid much attention to your feelings in this way, so the exercise is asking you to do something to which you aren't accustomed. Or perhaps at this particular moment nothing very obvious is happening in your emotional world. When this happens, don't give up. You're always having some kind of emotional experience, but it may be quite subtle or diffuse. Take a patient interest in whatever is there.

On some days, moving into the world of the emotions is like being a wildlife photographer. There is definitely life out there, but you need to be very still and watchful to begin to see it. If you can't identify any feelings, look for clues in your body that point to what might be going on. What is your breathing like? Is it calm and easy, or short and tight? How are your neck and shoulders? Your stomach? Noticing patterns of tension or relaxation, and especially the pleasant or unpleasant sensations that we explored in the previous exercise, will help you track down feelings that are subtle, or just coming to the surface.

The fourth exercise is more far-reaching. So far we have been exploring what has been going on within us, moment by moment, watching sensations in our body, watching feelings and emotions coming and going. Now we are going to explore our feeling responses to people, using our imagination to call them to mind. This is the last step in our preparation for practising loving-kindness meditation itself.

exercise 4 – responses to people

First, bring to mind someone you really like or love. Use your imagination to make them real to yourself in whatever way you can: see them in front of you, picture the way they move, hear the sound of their voice. Call to mind their mannerisms, or their characteristic phrases, or just get a kind of intuitive feel for their qualities and what they are like. Then just be aware of the feelings that arise when you are with this person in your imagination, right now.

Now let that person fade from your mind for the time being, and focus on someone you feel neutral about – you don't like or dislike them. This might be someone you have never got to know well but whom you see around: the postman or maybe a local shopkeeper, or it could be someone you know better but for whom you have no feelings either way: a work colleague or a friend of a friend. We all have interactions with people who, for one reason or another, don't push our emotional buttons (either the green ones or the red ones). Choose someone like that, bring them to mind, and watch your feelings. Anything happening? There could be luke-warm well-wishing, polite interest, a shrug of your inner shoulders, or irritation at the exercise. Don't set up any agendas about what you ought to be feeling. At this moment, the aim is just to experience whatever is there.

Let that second person fade away, and now bring to mind someone you don't like, or with whom you have difficulties. Again, don't get into old battles, recrimi-nations, or reciting your two page list of what is wrong with this person; just be aware of your feeling reaction. Notice what is going on in you, physically and emo-tionally, when you call this person onto the stage of your imagination. Do you tense up? Where? What is the feeling like when they appear? Again you may find it helpful to name the feeling, or to relate it to other experiences: a colour, a piece of music, a scent (or even a bad smell).

Once more, there is no need to be concerned by what-ever you find. Put yourself in the position of the wild-life photographer who might be taking pictures of a fearful gazelle or an enraged lioness. The aim is to cap-ture the moment as clearly and vividly as possible. Similarly, don't be concerned if you find that your emo-tion in relation to this person is fear, anger, or anything else. Just get to know the feeling. If you don't like it, this book will give you tools for working with it.

> *Now just let your mind roam, letting different people come to mind: all kinds of people, men and women of different backgrounds, nationalities, religions, and races. You can see them individually or in groups. All the time, keep your emotional radar on, noticing how you respond.*

> *Conclude by bringing your attention back to your physical experience. How does your body feel after that exercise? Then, in your own time, not rushing, open your eyes, take in the world around you, gently move a little, and then get up.*

There is a great deal to explore in each of these four exercises. If you practise them regularly you will build your capacity to be aware of what is happening to you on the feeling level. That has considerable benefits in itself. If you are not aware of the feelings that are driving you, you have no way of changing them. To change any mood or emotion you first have to get to know it. Continuing the wildlife analogy, if you don't know whether you are dealing with a gazelle or a lioness on the emotional level, if you can't tell a hoopoe from a hippo, then you won't have any chance of responding appropriately to what life brings you.

2

beginning to develop loving-kindness

So far, we have been exploring what's there in our experience, becoming more familiar with the ever-changing parade of our sensations, feelings, and emotions With that awareness as a basis, it is time to start working with the heart, to set up the conditions so that our feelings flow in a positive direction. In this chapter you will begin to learn a meditation that has been used by a huge number of people in the Buddhist tradition ever since the time of the Buddha, who himself recommended this practice.

Buddhist teachers use different phrases to describe the experience that this meditation develops.[4] Some call it friendliness, others call it loving-kindness. You could just call it love, which would be the simplest and strongest word. Unfortunately 'love' has become devalued. You can say 'I love my grandmother', but you can also say 'I love pizza' or 'I love it when I can get away from work early'. So I am going to talk in terms of loving-kindness. If you don't respond well to that term, don't let it put you off. We all know the kind of experience these different translations are referring to. It's an open-hearted state in which it feels as if a kind of inner sun has come out from behind the clouds and you feel loving, caring, and kind. If the term 'loving-kindness' doesn't invoke that feeling for you, just mentally replace it with one that does.

Now that we have a sense of what loving-kindness means in this context, we can begin to practise it in meditation. To make sure that we set off on the right track, we want to make the situation as straightforward as possible. So I suggest you bring to mind one or two friends who fulfil the following requirements:

They're roughly the same age as you – give or take ten or fifteen years. You might have been looking forward to practising this open-hearted meditation towards a favourite grandparent, or one of your children. Their time will come later. For now, we want a very simple feeling, and relationships between the generations are often coloured by complex issues. If you take someone of around your own age, the feeling is more likely to be one of equality.

They're alive, not dead. You can certainly practise this meditation towards deceased friends and relatives, but again that isn't where I suggest you start. When calling to mind people who have died, our feelings are often tinged with grief, or sometimes with emotional unfinished business. So for now we'll limit our choices to people who are alive.

You're not sexually attracted to them. Sorry to disappoint some of you! I'm not being a kind of puritan killjoy. It's just that we are looking for straightforward care and kindness. Although it is usually easier to feel good about someone attractive, which is why many politicians these days have expensive smiles, it wouldn't be helpful to pick someone for whom your feelings are mixed with desire and attachment. Also, meditating on someone to whom you're strongly attracted can degenerate into fantasies about what could happen if only they weren't married, or you were available, and so on.

If you can't think of anyone who fulfils these requirements exactly, then choose the person who comes closest. You might feel you don't have any good friends at the moment. In that case, think of someone with whom you would like to develop a friendship. In teaching this meditation I occasionally come across someone who claims they have no friends of around their own age, and still living, to whom they aren't attracted. If you're in that position (and I don't know whether to envy or pity you!) then you'll just have to do the best you can. Choose someone to whom you're not *very* attracted…

As your practice develops in the course of this book, you will be including all kinds of people, old and young, living and dead, attractive and unattractive. By then you will have gained a feeling for what loving-kindness is and what it isn't. Armed with that knowledge, you can spot it even when it is mixed with other feelings. For now, I hope you have found one or two people who fit the suggested requirements.

Make a mental note of them, and then decide on the one you will take for this meditation session. Once you have done that, you can start to practise opening your heart to them.

exercise 5 – loving-kindness meditation for a friend

Once again, begin by bringing a kindly awareness to your experience – first of your body and then of your feelings. Then call to mind the friend you have chosen. Make them as real in your imagination as you can. Be aware of them living their life just as you live yours. Hold them in your heart. What would they wish for themselves? They want their life to go well. They want to be healthy and happy, free from any kind of suffering. Deep down, at least, they want their life to be meaningful and fulfilling. So wish them all these things. If it feels helpful, you can put those wishes into words, internally repeating phrases like, 'May you be truly happy,' and 'May your life go really well.' Allow your feelings of care and appreciation to flow, and from that wish them well. Do this for as long as feels appropriate, then bring your attention back to your body and gently bring the meditation to an end.

So how was that for you? People doing this meditation for the first time respond in many different ways. Let's look at a few typical responses, and see what we can learn from them.

'My concentration came and went.' This is the case for the majority of people at first. It's how our minds are. Don't be perfectionist about this, feeling that you have to do it right. That will just get in the way. Take a lively interest in what happens, in what you notice.

Rather than giving yourself a hard time because you aren't doing what you are 'supposed' to do, celebrate those moments when you suddenly become aware that your mind has drifted off. Every moment of awareness is special and precious. You will find concentration becomes easier if you acknowledge and honour the times when you come back to awareness. Giving yourself a hard time for not concentrating is not within the meditation's spirit of loving-kindness. In fact it's counter-productive, as the mind doesn't respond well to being ordered around.

For some of us it would be easy to spend our lives responding to people's expectations. Meditation is one situation in which there need be no judgements, no success and failure. Give yourself a holiday from that whole way of being, and just allow yourself to be curious about what is happening, and the conditions that help to produce loving-kindness.

'I know I like my friend, but in the meditation I didn't feel anything for them.' Again, this may be a case of putting expectations onto the situation. People often imagine that in meditating on loving-kindness they will have some big, even cosmic, feeling of love – like their best romantic experience multiplied. But although with practice you might occasionally feel oceanic feelings of love – and not just for your good friend but for all that lives – most of the time your experience of loving-kindness is likely to be much more simple and low-key. If you had a feeling of your friend as another human being like you, and you felt that you *did* wish them well, then that will do nicely. If loving-kindness was a food it would be more like

rice and vegetables than strawberry cheesecake. Emotionally it can often feel quite simple, satisfying, and nourishing. Don't insist on whipping yourself up into some kind of Big Feeling. That is usually a sign that you don't have confidence in your own heart, your own feelings. You can trust them. Just give them time and awareness, and they will flower.

'I found I became absorbed in the meditation and wishing my friend well. It felt very expansive and satisfying.' Yes, it's like that sometimes. In fact, it can go very deep indeed. The human heart is a wonderful mystery, and when it opens life is suddenly very simple and profound at the same time. It's great when that happens; it's also fine if it doesn't. In the long run what counts is a kindly, steady effort each time you meditate. However you find your heart when you sit down and tune in to it, you aim to encourage it to open a little more. Then, with time, you will find love and kindness come more and more naturally and easily.

You can do this meditation, perhaps taking different friends who fit the criteria, as often as you like. Be honest with yourself about what you are feeling. You are not expected to develop 100% loving-kindness. At times you may be aware that your feelings of loving-kindness and friendliness are not very strong, or that they are mixed with all kinds of other emotions. That is quite natural, so don't let yourself be phased by it. Keep gently focusing on your friend, imagining what it is like to be in their shoes, feeling their hopes and aspirations, and wish them well.

3

five-stage meditation

So far, we have been practising the development of loving-kindness towards a friend, which is a natural place to start. We like our friends, and it is usually not hard to wish them well, unless some other feelings such as jealousy or competitiveness get in the way. But in the Buddhist view we can widen out that feeling of friendliness and well-wishing indefinitely, including more and more human beings, and even animals and other forms of life. This may seem like a tall order, but we can do it step by step, and with practice open our hearts more and more.

In this chapter I'm going to describe a way of meditating in five stages.[5] It is like a gym routine: a complete workout for your positive emotions, which you develop by focusing on individuals you have different kinds of feelings for, and then stretch to include more and more living beings. This structured approach is progressive; once your heart is warmed up in the first couple of stages, it has to work harder and expand more in the later ones. But, as we'll see, this 'work' is actually very gentle and unforced.

Let's start with an overview of the five stages.

> Stage 1 – Yourself
>
> Stage 2 – A good friend
>
> Stage 3 – Someone you feel neutral about
>
> Stage 4 – Someone you are finding difficult
>
> Stage 5 – All four people together, then widening out more and more to other people all around the world, and finally to all forms of life.

If you did the exercise at the end of Chapter 1, you will recognize this sequence. In that exercise we were just calling people to mind and acknowledging our feelings about them. Here we are going a stage further. We shall still begin by acknowledging what our feelings are, but then we shall gently work to find and develop feelings of kindness and friendliness.

The practice begins very close to home, with you. From there it moves on to someone you naturally tend to feel good towards, then someone you have no particular feelings for, followed by someone you find difficult or actively dislike. So in stages 2 to 4 we work with people who tend to provoke in us pleasant, neutral, and unpleasant feelings respectively. By practising this meditation over time, we learn to go beyond having our responses dominated by these feelings, and to wish all these human beings well. In the final stage, we start by developing equanimity (we'll see what that means later), then we expand the circle of loving-kindness, including more and more people. We can take this last stage as far as we like, sending love to people everywhere, and even to animals, birds, and so on. So in the course of the meditation we move from ourselves at the centre of our world, through individuals who represent people who play different parts in our world, then outwards more and more, opening our heart (on a good day when the practice goes well) to the whole world.

We'll look at the five stages of the meditation in turn, and then I'll talk you through a session of practice.

In the first stage you look for and develop feelings of love and care for yourself. The more you are on good terms with yourself and wish yourself well, the easier it will be to send loving-kindness to others. Many of us don't like ourselves very much, or suffer from low self-esteem. If you do this meditation regularly, it can really change that. In a way, just the decision to meditate can already be an expression of kindness for yourself. You have given yourself this time to meditate, to explore and enhance your experience. Just sitting down and spending time in this way is a statement that you value and care for yourself.

We twenty-first-century dwellers often rush from one thing to the next, responding to all kinds of needs around us, and don't do a good job of meeting our own deeper needs. When we do give to ourselves, it is often something that will not really nourish us. We slump in front of the TV or the computer, eat chocolate for comfort, or have one coffee too many. However, what really nourishes us as human beings is to be alive in the moment, awake in our experience, and to experience positive emotions such as love and kindness – whether from people around us or generated in our own hearts. This first stage of the meditation directly addresses these deeper needs. It will give you greater resources to deal with your life, and to respond to what it asks of you.

If the first stage can be tricky because of our ambivalence towards ourselves, the second stage is often much more straightforward. As usual, to help keep things straightforward, you choose someone who is alive, roughly the same age as you, and to whom you aren't particularly sexually attracted. Because your positive feelings about your friend give you a head start in developing a feeling of loving-kindness, you can often build up quite a strong feeling in this stage. You then move on to people you find less easy.

In the third stage you select someone you don't feel strongly about. You don't feel particularly good about them, they aren't someone you can't stand, they're just another human being. They might be someone who works in the corner store, another parent you see when you pick up your child from school, or someone at work whom you don't know much about. So you are starting from scratch in terms of feeling for this person, but you have the momentum from the first two stages to help you.

Then in the fourth stage you take on a real challenge. You choose someone you find difficult. This is a person who, when you call them to mind, brings up unpleasant feelings in you. It could be anger or fear, frustration or annoyance. In principle this could be a real enemy. If someone murdered your grandmother or ran off with your lover, they will fall naturally into the fourth stage. But as a newcomer to this meditation, it would probably be asking too much of yourself to take on your all-time difficult person, the one who blighted your life, and try to find friendly feelings for them. It is better to start with an easier subject. As your capacity for love and forgiveness grows, through doing this practice over time, you can work up to people who really make you mad, or cause you to feel really bad about yourself.

So when you're learning this meditation, choose someone whom you're currently finding a bit hard going. It could be someone who is usually a friend, but with whom you've had a misunderstanding. Or it might be someone who irritates or annoys you. The feeling doesn't have to be mutual. This person might feel perfectly OK towards you. They might not even realize there is any problem. It may be that you think they're fine as a person too, but somehow you don't feel good towards them. When you examine your feeling you may recognize that you're a bit jealous, or feeling competitive with them.

The final stage has two parts. (You could even think of six stages, but we'll follow tradition and talk in terms of five.) In the first, shorter part you call to mind all the four people you have meditated on so far. You imagine them together, and notice how you are feeling towards each of them after the earlier stages. You see which person you feel most friendly towards, and gently work to open your heart to the others in the same way. The ideal here (and we're real people who don't usually live up to ideals, but they give us something to aim for, a direction) is to reach a point where you feel equally strongly towards all four. This equality of feeling – which isn't bland, it's strong towards each of you – we can call equanimity. So if all four of you were seated round a dinner table, and there was only one extra portion of something very tasty, you would be perfectly relaxed and at ease, because you wouldn't mind which of you ate it.

Once you've spent a little time doing what you can to find equanimity in relation to the four people from the earlier stages, you start doing something extra-ordinary. You widen out the feeling to include an ever-increasing number of men and women. Like dropping a stone in a pool and watching ripples going out in all directions, you let the circle of loving-kindness and well-wishing expand and expand. You can do this as much as you like, until you are holding endless numbers of people in your heart. Obviously you won't be able to call them to mind individually. You might just think of 'all the people in California' or even 'all the people in Africa'. You could never get to know them all, but you can still wish them all well, all these human beings going about their lives.

You needn't stop there. You can include other life on this planet, from your pet dog or cat outwards, to include fish, birds, mammals, reptiles, and insects. Everything under the sun can be embraced by your feeling of friendliness and loving-kindness. Or even under other suns: if you believe there may be life on other planets, or in other dimensions of consciousness, you can include them too. In the Buddhist tradition, this meditation is one of a set known as the immeasurables. Through this practice you can potentially open your heart to measureless numbers of beings, to all life wherever it may be.

To help you to get a feel for it, I'll guide you through a session of this five-stage meditation.

a guided meditation
Begin as you have been, by sitting down and finding a comfortable but upright position. Let your posture express the dignity of being human and doing something really worthwhile. Before you start the meditation, choose three people whom you can call to mind in the second, third, and fourth stages (for the second stage, remembering to choose a friend of roughly your own age, who is alive, and who you don't find sexually attractive).

Gently close your eyes and turn your attention to your body. Take a kindly interest in it. How is it now? Allow yourself to explore it without expectations, with a gentle curiosity. When you have a sense of it, focus for a few moments on the sensation of your bottom on your chair or cushion. (If you're on a chair, you can also take your awareness down to the soles of your feet.) Have a sense of the earth, solid beneath you. Relax and give your weight to it. Allow yourself to enjoy that sense of being supported by the earth.

From that sense of groundedness and relaxation in your lower body, allow your spine to gently rise up – not stiff and tight, but as if the crown of your head were attached to a balloon which lifted it just enough to create some freedom in the spine, a sense of spaciousness between the vertebrae. This upward movement of the crown of your head also has the effect of slightly tucking in your chin. Savour the feeling of sitting well, relaxed but alive and alert.

Now bring your awareness to your heart centre – to that place in the centre of your chest that feels it is involved when you feel kind and loving. It is the place that you naturally feel when you hear or say a phrase like 'my heart goes out to them' or 'with all my heart'. With a very kindly awareness, explore what you feel there. Try to let go of judgements and expectations, just 'listen' to what is happening there.

If you feel nothing is going on, just wait patiently, with curiosity, and lower your expectations. There is always some feeling, but you may be looking for something more dramatic than what is there. Really tune in to that place. If you still don't notice anything, pay attention to pleasant or painful sensations in your body for clues to what you might be feeling.

Once you have focused your attention, with a very kindly awareness in your heart centre, begin to focus on that awareness itself. Allow it to become a feeling of kindness for yourself, really wishing yourself well. If it helps, you can say silently to yourself, 'May I be happy,' 'May my life go well,' or other phrases that might come to you. Don't repeat them mechanically. Say one and allow it to percolate through your being. Feel how you respond to it.

If you find yourself closed to wishing yourself well or expressing kindness to yourself, just be aware of that.

It's very common to feel unworthy or undeserving of love, or to feel that opening your heart is a risk in some way. Don't worry about it. Just put loving-kindness around whatever you're feeling. After all, someone who finds it difficult to feel much for themselves really needs kindness and love, don't they?

Keep focusing on your heart and wishing yourself well, enfolding whatever is happening in your experience in a kindly awareness.

Now invite into that 'heart space' a friend you feel good about. Do what you can to get a sense of them: be aware of how they look, the clothes they wear, their voice, their laugh, their qualities, the kind of atmosphere they create when they come into a room. Gently hold them in your heart. View them with kindness, appreciating how your life would be poorer if you didn't know them. Just as you wished yourself well, take some time to wish them well too.

When you're ready, call to mind someone you feel neutral about. Make them as vivid for yourself as you can. Reflect on how, in many ways, they are just like you. This very moment, like you, they are breathing, their heart is beating, and they are experiencing various feelings. Like you, they want to be happy, not un-happy, and they have hopes and fears about how their lives are turning out. Be sensitive to your heart, and see what its response is to your awareness of your common humanity. See if you can wish them well on the basis of that feeling of human solidarity.

When the time feels right, turn your mind to someone you find difficult in some way. As you do this, keep a kindly awareness of what is happening in your body. Perhaps even imagining this person is enough to cause you to tense up. See if you can allow yourself to relax, to let go of the fight or flight response, and simply view this person objectively. We all have people with whom the dynamics are difficult: people we don't understand, or with whom we somehow can't get on the same wavelength. This person probably has friends and family, people who think they are OK. So they are not just a 'bad person'. Also, even the meanest and nastiest behaviour stems from some deep sense of unsatisfactoriness, of frustration, of buried pain. See if, reflecting in this way, you can open your heart to this person. Don't compromise your integrity. You don't have to pretend you really like them, or overlook your issues with them. But maybe you can see beyond the difficulties to a wider sense of them as a person. Do you actually want them to suffer? See what your heart's response is to that. Try wishing them well, and free from suffering. (They would probably be a nicer person then.) Allow yourself to be big enough, your heart to be open enough, to put aside what stands in the way and, at least in the privacy of your own mind, to be friendly and caring towards them.

Now call to mind the people you have been meditating on, and imagine all three together with you – maybe in a circle. Consult your heart again: who do you feel the most for? And the least? Notice how it is enjoyable to feel more love and care rather than less. Allow your heart to open to all four of you, so that the feeling becomes stronger for those for whom you didn't feel so much. You might find this easier if you focus on your common humanity, and get a sense of solidarity between the four of you on that basis. Don't be concerned if there is still quite a discrepancy in how much you feel for different individuals. Being perfectionist isn't very kind to yourself.

When you have equalized the feeling as best you can, allow it to expand outwards, opening your heart to more and more people. Start close to home: anyone in your building, then everyone in your street, then your neighbourhood. Now let the warm feelings of love and friendliness widen out, like ripples on a lake.

Include everyone in your area, then everyone in the country where you live, the continent, other continents, all the oceans, the whole world. Open your heart to other forms of life: mammals, birds, insects, and so on – all the forms of life that share our planet. May they all be well and happy, may they all be free from suffering. Don't even stop there. Throw open the doors of your heart to the whole universe, wherever there could be life of any kind. Let it all be pervaded by loving-kindness and well-wishing.

When the time feels right, bring the focus of your attention back to your body. Feel your connection to the ground. Give yourself a little time to assimilate the effects of the meditation. Then slowly open your eyes, take in your surroundings, and, when you're ready, get up.

regular practice
For best results, this meditation should be done regularly. If you can make the time, then 20 or 25 minutes

is a good period to aim for. That is long enough to give you a chance to tune in to your feelings and wish yourself well, to spend a few minutes with people in the second, third, and fourth stages, and still have some time to equalize and radiate the feeling. (Don't spend too long on equalizing; it's usually best to spend most of the time in the last stage widening out the feeling.) But do what you can do. Even five minutes will have an effect on your mind and leave your heart a little more open. It is usually best to go through all the stages, but if you are really short of time you could just do the first one or two, then briefly expand the feeling out to the world.

If you have things to do, and you're worried that you might meditate for too long, you can time yourself using a watch or clock. If you're sitting with your eyes closed you can occasionally open them for a moment or two to check how long you have left (although regular meditators usually develop a pretty accurate sense of how much time has elapsed).

You can also 'top up' the meditation at odd moments in the day. For instance, at work, you can occasionally take a break for a minute or two to wish yourself well and then send love out into the world around you. Doing this will refresh your mind and help you to keep in touch with the feeling of the meditation throughout the day.

4

starting and finishing well

It is important to begin and end a meditation session well. Meditation takes place in a deeper and more concentrated state of mind than everyday consciousness. To give yourself the best chance of accessing a deeper state, it is best to go into it step by step, setting up the conditions for it to happen. Similarly, at the end of the meditation you need to retrace your steps from the meditative world to everyday consciousness. It can feel very jarring and unpleasant if you just leap up and try to do the next thing. Here is a suggested routine for leading yourself into and out of meditation on loving-kindness.

starting to meditate
Begin the meditation by doing your best to ensure you will not be disturbed for about 20 minutes. Find a comfortable way to sit. For meditation you need to find a position in which you can relax but keep your back straight. In this way, your physical posture will

encourage the mental state that you are looking for in meditation: relaxed but wide awake and alert. To achieve this posture you can sit on a straight-backed chair, on cushions, or kneel using a stool. (If you start practising regularly, it is worth investing in cushions, or a stool, specifically designed for meditation.) It is possible to meditate lying down, but doing so will increase the chances of becoming drowsy, so I wouldn't recommend it if you can sit comfortably instead.

Talking of drowsiness, it is usually best to meditate with your eyes closed, but if you are tired you may prefer to keep them half-open, gazing unfocused at the ground a few feet in front of you.

Once you have found a comfortable but alert posture, it is good to reflect on your reasons for meditating – which may change from day to day. What really motivates you, right now, to want to develop loving-kindness for yourself, for your family and friends, for the world? Like any activity, meditation doesn't go well when you have no positive sense of why you are doing it, or the benefits you will gain from it. So it is worth taking a minute or two to find what inspires you to do it. Some activities like brushing your teeth can be done on autopilot, but meditation is all about being present in the moment, alive to what is happening. You won't find that aliveness unless you are interested and motivated.

Then briefly review what you are going to do. If you are not used to this five-stage meditation, you can remind yourself of the five stages. You can also decide now which people you are going to put in the second, third, and fourth stages. (You might prefer to do this intuitively at the beginning of those stages, but thinking 'shall I pick him or her?' can be distracting during the actual meditation.)

After that, become aware of your physical body. This helps to ground you in the present moment, your present experience. You can either tune in to various sensations as they present themselves, or you can systematically scan through your body, from head to toe, being aware of how it feels. You can note things like pleasant or unpleasant feelings, temperature, degree of tension or relaxation, and a sense of energy flowing through your body. Where you feel tense, you can take a kindly interest in your experience, inviting the tension to release. (But don't insist on the tension disappearing; forcing yourself to relax is counterproductive!)

Finally, take an interest in how you are feeling. Acknowledge what is there. Even if it feels a long way away from loving-kindness, it is still your experience in this moment. Turn towards it with as much friendliness and interest as you can muster. Hold whatever you are feeling with kindly awareness. Doing so should lead you naturally into the first stage of the practice.

ending the practice

Once you have gone through the five stages, and opened your heart to as many living beings as you can, it is time to emerge from the meditation.

Stop making any effort and just experience the state in which the meditation has left you. Let go of the meditation. Just sit with the feelings that have been developed by the practice. Sitting with this broad awareness is very helpful for absorbing the effects of what you have just done.

Bring your attention to your body. If you have become absorbed in sending out friendliness and kindly feelings to the world, you might not have had much sense of your physical body. During the meditation, that is quite OK. It is like when you watch a film, you may not notice your body at all, unless something shocking happens and you catch your breath or your heart starts beating rapidly. But the body is your anchor in the everyday world, so becoming aware of it is an excellent way of grounding yourself after the meditation. Be aware of how it feels, all the different sensations.

If you have been sitting with eyes closed, now gently open them, and give yourself a few seconds to take in your surroundings.

Next, move and stretch. Don't do this too vigorously. Meditation, when it goes well, brings about deep relaxation. So afterwards it is good to stretch, just as you might naturally do when you wake in the morning.

Finally, get up and move on to your next activity. If possible, rather than rushing straight into things, give yourself a few minutes of transition: do something simple that doesn't require much thought, like making a drink, watering your plants, or taking a short walk.

Meditation can be deceptive. Sometimes at the end of a loving-kindness session it will be clear that something has happened. You will be very relaxed, or you may notice that when you get up at the end the world looks brighter and sharper. At other times you might feel you weren't very concentrated, or you couldn't contact much in the way of friendliness or love. Even if you feel nothing happened, still take your time to emerge from the meditation. It is hard to judge the depth of a meditation. Sometimes you might be surprised to discover that although you thought you weren't very concentrated, it takes a while to come back to the everyday world. And if you did spend the whole time with your mind whizzing and whirring, it will be helpful if you take the time to experience that, and then feel the body gently stretch, and take in your surroundings before you get up. Doing this will slow you down and put you more in contact with your experience.

5

expressing the feeling

Now that you have learned the five-stage method of loving-kindness meditation, and a helpful routine for beginning and ending a session, you have laid the foundations for an ongoing practice of meditation on the heart. In the next three chapters I'll give you a toolkit, or palette – whichever image you prefer – of methods you can use to make it more effective. For the practice to go well, you need two elements that we haven't really looked at so far: ways to contact and encourage the feeling of loving-kindness, and ways to make your sense of the people in the second and later stages as vivid as possible.

This chapter and the next will help you with contacting and expressing friendliness and loving-kindness. In Chapter 7 we'll look at how to give yourself a strong sense of connection with the people you are meditating on. I'll just mention here that to help connect with a sense of the person, you can call to mind a mental picture, the sound of their voice, their name, any characteristic mannerisms or things associated with them, or any combination of all these. For now, let's assume you have developed some sense of the person you are focusing on, and look at ways of contacting and expressing positive feeling for them. We'll look at six methods, involving phrases, light, heat, images, the body, and memories. (To keep things simple, in the exercises in this chapter we'll focus again on a good friend, but these methods all work very well in the later meditation stages as well.)

phrases

One very effective way to develop the feeling is to find words to express what you wish for, and then let them echo in the silence of your heart. There are a number of phrases traditionally used to express loving-kindness in this way. Here are three of them:

'May you be well.'

'May you be happy.'

'May you be free from suffering.'

A fourth phrase that is often added is something like, 'May you make progress on the path (to Awakening),' because it is through maturing as a human being and understanding the nature of life that we start to overcome suffering. You're welcome to use this phase or, if it doesn't feel right, you could find your own version, or just stick with the first three.

Phrases like these can give a focus to what you are feeling, and also help to draw out more feeling. It's like when you say something to someone, perhaps rather tentatively, and discover through saying it out loud that you *really* feel or believe it.

You can silently repeat one or more of the phrases to yourself. If you do this, it's important to allow it to be quite spacious, and to focus on the feeling the words are conveying. Otherwise you can end up parroting the phrases without any feeling. At that point your mind will become bored and wander off. Five minutes later you may realize that you have been thinking about something else entirely while still saying to yourself, 'May you be well.'

This exercise goes best when you manage to maintain a dual focus. Part of you is aware of the person you are wishing well; the other is on your feeling. The phrase is the communication link between the two. Think of a time when you really wanted to communicate something to another person. Perhaps you looked them in the eye and said, 'I love you.' Even if it was, 'I don't love you any more,' or, 'Leave me alone,' the principle is the same. In that moment you were strongly in touch with your feeling and very aware of the other person, and you sent a few words, very focused and direct, from your heart straight to them. Saying these phrases internally won't be as dramatic or highly-charged, but see if you can allow it to have those same ingredients – your feeling, your awareness of the other person, and the short phrase that is like a spark arcing across the space to express your feeling to them.

exercise 6 – finding your own phrases

In this exercise, prepare to meditate, and then bring to mind a close friend. Make them as vivid for yourself as you can, and allow feelings of loving-kindness to flow out to them. This time, rather than using the trad-itional phrases, see if you can find your own words to express your feeling. There are no prizes for original-ity, and you don't need to come up with some long, complex appreciation. You aren't giving a wedding speech, and anything too complex may take you away from the underlying feeling. Just tune in to your friend and your positive feeling for them. Put your awareness into that heart feeling and let it speak. It is almost as if the everyday 'you' stands to one side for a few moments and allows that deeper part to speak through you.

If your mind is blank and no phrases come up, go back to the traditional ones for the time being. But be open to the possibility of something of your own popping up.

If there really is a whole flow of words, that's fine. But in general a short phrase is enough. Let it echo in the silence of your heart. Keep paying attention to the feel-ing. You may find that producing the phrase has changed it in some way. See if there is another phrase that wants to be expressed. If not, repeat the phrase you just used, or stay with the silence.

When you're ready, bring your awareness to your body, then open your eyes and take in the outer world.

You don't have to use your own phrases. (In fact you don't have to use phrases at all.) It's fine to stick to the traditional ones; in a way, they say it all. But it can open up new aspects of the practice if you allow a spontaneous flow of well-wishing to find its own appropriate words. This can be particularly helpful if you have got into a bit of a rut with the practice.

One thing I've discovered over the years is that it is good if the phrases are not too specific. Wishes made with a concentrated mind are powerful. They have effects beyond what we expect. In my life I notice that I have usually gained or attained what I have wished for. The only problem is that a lot of what I wished for wasn't very wise. It is very hard to know how life will turn out, and what will make us happy, let alone what would be really fulfilling for someone else. So rather than wishing for someone, 'May you become vastly wealthy and live in a huge house,' it would be better to wish, 'May you have the perfect living situation for you.' That is why the traditional phrases are limited to wishing for things that would be good for anyone: good health, happiness, freedom from suffering, and deepening maturity as a human being. By all means make the phrases specific to the person: 'May your arthritis improve,' 'May you be free from worry and anxiety,' and so on. But don't use phrases that imply that you know the best lifestyle, partner, job, religious or political affiliation, etc. that will make them happy. Life and people are deep and mysterious, and sometimes things turn out well in ways that none of us could have predicted.

light
Light has a very powerful effect on our emotions. Sunshine and blue sky usually make us feel more open and expansive. The same is true of our inner world. So one way to connect with loving-kindness for a friend is to imagine sending them light. Whatever the colour of the light you send, let it be very warm, like sunlight, an expression of your feeling.

exercise 7 – sending light

In this meditation, begin as usual, calling to mind a good friend, making them vivid for you, and contacting your positive feeling for them. Imagine your feelings of care and well-wishing going out to them as light. The light can be any colour that feels appropriate to you. Use your intuition. If you're not sure, then try different colours – but see if you can do it while staying in touch with your friend and the feeling. What is the best colour match for how you feel for them? Or you could ask yourself what colour would be appropriate for them and what they need now. Bathe your friend in light for as long as you like, then come back and focus on your own heart for a short while before bringing the meditation to a close.

heat

It's interesting that loving-kindness definitely has temperature associated with it. Look at words like 'heart-warming'. Or when someone says, 'I felt bathed in love,' they usually have a sense of light and heat, as if love was like a kind of liquid sunshine, warming and relaxing them. So when you send waves of loving-kindness to your friend, there is often a sense of physical warmth associated with that. By focusing on that warmth, you can make the feeling of well-wishing more tangible. This exercise focuses on raising the emotional temperature.

exercise 8 – the warmth of loving-kindness

Once again move into the space of meditation, bring your friend vividly to mind, and allow your heart to open to them. When you are in touch with a friendly

> *and loving feeling, see if you can experience that as a kind of warmth in your heart. As you keep focusing on your friend and your heart's response to them, do you notice an increase in the amount of heat in your heart radiating out to them? Keep focusing on your friend and on your loving-kindness as heat. Allow its warmth to bathe your friend like sunshine. Let this happen for as long as you like, and then finish the meditation in the usual way.*

'Warm-heartedness' isn't just a metaphor. The heat of friendliness, love, and well-wishing can become a very definite physical experience. On a very good meditation day, you might even feel your heart as a kind of furnace of loving-kindness. But if it's not like that today, don't be discouraged or hard on yourself. Over time, this practice will definitely warm your heart. You just have to keep going.

images

There are many ways in which you can harness the power of your imagination to help make the practice more effective. In the first stage, as an expression of kindness and wishing yourself well, you can imagine yourself in a state of well-being, or feeling very open-hearted. You can promote the feeling of loving-kindness for others by seeing your heart as an open lotus or other flower. It can also help if you imagine others being well and happy.

Another way I sometimes use images in the meditation is as a way of describing and transforming feelings. For instance, as I start by becoming aware of how I am feeling, I may notice that I am a bit closed in on myself and my energy isn't flowing very well. One way in which I can work with this is to find an image that sums up my experience. It might be of being in a dark cell, of being locked up in myself. Or it might be of a tight belt around my midriff preventing me from breathing easily. When I have found an image that feels like a good equivalent of my state, I ask myself what would change it for the better. I might introduce a window or an open door into the cell, or vividly imagine releasing the belt a few notches.

I find this kind of work with images can change my state quite markedly, and make it much easier to develop feelings of friendliness for myself. In the same way, I can find an image for my relationships with the people that I put in the other stages, and work with them. I wouldn't advocate doing this in every meditation, but it is a good way of clearing the decks when difficult feelings – either physical or emotional – are standing between you and the experience of loving-kindness.

My only reservation about the use of imagination is that people sometimes use it as a way to avoid their feelings. When you sit down to meditate one day you might be feeling quite low and down. You could respond to this with some fantasy in which you are feeling very happy and doing something like swimming with dolphins. The question is, are you using that fantasy as a creative way of working with your feelings and changing your state, or are you off with the dolphins as a way of avoiding the truth of your experience?

the body

Involving your body in the meditation is very effective, as it helps to keep you grounded. It is particularly effective in the first stage. From the moment you sit down and set up your posture, you can be developing kindness for yourself. If you look at images of the Buddha or other Buddhist figures, they often convey a sense of confidence and dignity. In practising this meditation you are following in their footsteps, so you can sit like a Buddha: upright, relaxed, with your chest open. This will help you develop a sense of self-confidence and open-heartedness, as well as the dignity of someone who is working to become more loving and a friend to the world.

You can also imagine your body as full of energy, or call to mind what your physical experience was like at times when you felt really happy and alive. It can be helpful, too, to be aware of what happens to your energy as you focus on your heart and start to wish yourself well. Through doing this you can at times be aware of subtle releases of energy in your body.

Another way of using the body to assist the flow of loving-kindness is by letting yourself smile a little. Even if you don't feel particularly like smiling, acting as if you were feeling friendly and loving can help to evoke those feelings. You can use it in the first stage to help you tune in to a feeling of loving-kindness, and then you can greet everyone you meet in the later stages of the meditation with a smile too. At times that will feel fine; at others it might feel dishonest. If allowing yourself a smile feels wrong, given how you are feeling at present, then at least see if you can relax the muscles of your face and jaw.

memories

We talked earlier about ways of making someone vivid – being aware of a sense of their presence, how they look, their voice, characteristic mannerisms, or their name. In doing that, you are using the power of memory to call to mind the person in the present. But you can also draw on memories from the past to help draw up positive feelings. This exercise will give you an idea of how you can do this.

exercise 9 – recalling the good times

In this exercise, move into meditation, spend a few minutes wishing yourself well, then call to mind a good friend. Once you have a sense of them, recall times you've spent with them that have been enjoyable or meaningful. Call to mind any occasions when they were helpful to you: maybe they rallied round at a difficult time, or perhaps they just bought you an ice cream on a hot day. As you relive these positive memories, notice any feelings of appreciation or gratitude that arise. Gently home in on them, and allow them to fuel your feeling of friendliness and well-wishing. Do this for as long as you like, and then bring the meditation to a close.

combining some of the above

So far, we've looked at involving different senses in the meditation. The phrases use ideas and inner sound. The light and imagery use inner sight. Working with the body, developing a sense of warmth, and radiating light or heat also use inner senses. I suppose in theory you could also use taste or smell. I haven't seen it suggested in any of the old Buddhist texts, but if you want to try something new after 2,500 years then you could experiment with connecting loving-kindness with a beautiful scent and let it waft from your heart. If loving-kindness was a scent, what would it be?

As human beings, we are very good at multitasking with the senses, so you can also combine different methods. This often happens naturally. I sometimes find that as I am using phrases there is also a sense of light or warmth going out to my friend. See if combining phrases and imagery works for you.

As I mentioned, all these different methods work well in the later stages as well as in the second – though you might not have any positive memories to draw on for the people in the third and fourth stages. As for the first stage, you can certainly use phrases, imagery, and working with your body. Imagining healing light and/or warmth pouring from your heart and filling your body is very effective. You can also recall times when you were at your best, or when you helped others, in order to increase your feelings of positive self-esteem and make it easier to wish yourself well.

Whatever methods you use, you will probably find that the strength of your feeling varies. It comes in bursts, or in waves. Feeling can sometimes be a bit like your sense of smell. If you go out into a garden where there is something strongly-scented, your nose will pick it out and delight in it. But very quickly your brain 'tunes out' the scent, so that you don't experience it so strongly. You may have to walk away and then come back to the plant to get another full-strength appreciation of the richness of what is there. It is the same with feelings of loving-kindness; they are likely to wax and wane, and you may need to try different ways of helping them to flow. So, over time, it would be good to explore all the suggestions in this chapter, so that you have several tools at your disposal.

6

heart of hearts

All the methods we learned in the previous chapter can be helpful ways of giving tangible expression (as tangible as things get in the subtle inner world of meditation) to your feeling of friendliness and well-wishing. However, it is possible to become too caught up with techniques. You can play around with them and lose touch with why you are meditating. Playfulness is a helpful quality to develop, but superficiality isn't. The question to ask yourself with all these different ways of doing the practice is always: is this helping me to contact and deepen a feeling of loving-kindness?

People who are learning to meditate often become overly concerned with techniques. When I first learned this practice I wasn't given many alternative ways of doing it. I received basic instruction in the meditation in five stages and some traditional phrases to work with. That was it. This meant that my range of ways of working in the meditation was very limited, but it had the advantage that I had to focus on the core aims of the practice. I didn't have much chance to keep chopping and changing, using different techniques all the time.

All Buddhist meditations are designed to help you escape from suffering. Not to be escapist, but genuinely to arrive at a way of being in which mental suffering is reduced or even eliminated. Some forms of meditation might suit one person more than another, but they will all have that effect if you sincerely practise them for long enough. In that sense, our situation is a bit like being a prisoner of war: we have no mental freedom, and the meditation is like a method of tunnelling your way out. One tunnel may take you east, another takes you west, one may go through slightly tougher soil, but they will all take you beyond the guards and the perimeter wire to freedom. All you have to do is choose a method, a place to start, and keep working on the practice, keep on digging.

However, remembering what I was like during my early years of meditation, and watching others over the years, I can see the same frustrating pattern. I would start digging east, and make good progress for a while, but then it would become harder. Big stones, tough work. At that point, instead of keeping going, albeit at a much slower pace, I would assume that I was digging in the wrong direction. I'd stop tunnelling east and start going north instead. After a while, I would hit another a rough phase. So I'd try going west. If I could show you an image of my mind after a few years of practice, it would look like a rabbit warren. Tunnels everywhere, all abandoned when the going got a bit tough with the idea that it shouldn't be like that, and I must be doing something wrong.

By all means use phrases, imagery, light, memories – anything you like – but be careful about assuming that when the meditation isn't going well the thing to do is to reach for another technique. Sometimes that will help, but trying another technique will often be just superficial tinkering. What you really need to do is move below that surface level of your experience. In this chapter we shall look at some exercises for tuning in to a deeper level of experience, a level on which love and friendliness flow much more easily and naturally. We shall learn to listen to our heart.

By 'heart' here I don't mean the physical pump inside your chest, but that sense of an inner 'place' that is indicated by phrases like 'we had a real heart to heart' or 'in my heart of hearts'. Most people, when they use phrases like that, will feel that in some way the experience is connected with the area in the middle of the chest, back from their breastbone. Yet this 'heart', which feels very central to who we are, isn't a physical location. Somehow it is on a deeper, more inward level of our experience.

exercise 10 – listening to your heart

Prepare yourself as you would for any meditation, starting by finding a posture in which you are relaxed and alert. Now look for some interest and enthusiasm for doing the exercise – which here will probably mean developing a sense of curiosity about what 'listening to your heart' means, and what could come out of doing it. As usual, the next stage is to anchor yourself in the

present moment by focusing on your body and its sen-
sations, and then to see what you can notice about how
you are feeling.

Once you have well prepared in this way, begin gently
to explore the experience of your heart. Listen in the
direction of that 'inner place' from which your deepest
feelings and greatest integrity seem to flow. If it helps,
you can quietly say to yourself 'in my heart of hearts',
or use a memory of a real 'heart meeting' with someone.

Listen without expectation of any particular response.
The main thing is that you are turning towards that
deep level of your experience and being open to it.
Again, it might help if you listen with a kind of word-
less question (if that makes any sense to you). If it were
put into words it might be something like, 'How is it
with my heart now?' Listen with as much receptivity
as you can muster, and see what you experience in
response. That response might be feelings, words,
images, sensations – all kinds of things are possible. It
might be very definite, quite unclear, or apparently
nothing at all.

Continue listening to your heart until it feels time to
bring the exercise to an end. Come out of it by following
the steps at the end of Chapter 4.

It's important to do this exercise without trying to
achieve any particular result. The purpose isn't to
come back bearing some trophy from this expedition
into your inner world. The exercise is about learning
to be open and receptive to a deeper level of your being, to begin building a bridge of awareness between
the everyday you and your core feeling and knowing.

While the last exercise was more intuitive, the next one involves reflecting on your experience in order to test out some of your views about yourself. So often we are suspicious of ourselves and our motives, feeling that we are not really very kind or compassionate. The aim of this exercise is to challenge some of those assumptions and give you greater confidence in your heart and your care for other people.

exercise 11 – *natural goodness*

> *Take some time to reflect on your experience of how you respond when you hear about some suffering in the world. What is your first natural response to hearing that people have been killed in an earthquake, or that an acquaintance has been hurt in a car accident? Do you feel blank, concerned, or anxious?*
>
> *If you somehow had the power to put an end to all the suffering in the world, would you want to do it?*

I suspect that through doing this exercise you will find that you are naturally moved and saddened by suffering, and that if you could alleviate it you would. That seems to be our most fundamental human response. However, it can easily become covered over by other feelings. Sometimes we are too stressed, too busy struggling with our own lives, to feel very much. Or sometimes the suffering of others scares us, reminding us that we and those we love are also, sooner or later, going to suffer. So we respond with a kind of horrified anxiety that gets in the way of a simple open-hearted feeling. Most often, I believe, our natural compassion is blocked by a sense of powerlessness. We hear of some tragedy and feel there is nothing we can do about it. It is very painful to watch others suffer and be unable to help. Rather than experience the pain of that, we shut off and close our heart. This closing-off often happens quickly and automatically. As a result, we come to believe we are not very caring and compassionate. That is why it is helpful to ask yourself the question about whether you would alleviate suffering if you really had the power to do so. It helps you be aware of your natural desire that people and animals should not suffer, and gives you a better and truer sense of the goodness of your own heart.

I once proposed a thought experiment to a roomful of people to whom I was teaching meditation. I suggested that if the world had been created by a supreme being (which isn't the Buddhist view), it had all the signs of a botched job. In fact it was probably designed by a committee. I suggested that the forty of us were that committee, the design team of Galactic Origin and Design. It was now time for us to review how our design had worked out. I reminded the committee that, as usual, this project had been run to a very tough deadline and an unrealistic budget, so it wasn't surprising that a number of errors had crept in, resulting in warfare, disease, famine, and other unintended events. But our team of programmers and engineers had been working hard to come up with fixes for the various design faults. While sadly we couldn't do anything about past sufferings (GOD's lawyers and financial advisers were busy preparing for the resulting lawsuits that were likely to be filed against the corporation) we could now agree to put the revised design in place to produce a completely suffering-free environment. All those in favour?

Forty hands went up. Passed with no abstentions.

It is important to keep in touch with that simple, natural response of your heart, and to trust that it is there in others too. When you are in touch with it, the meditation flows more easily and naturally.

In the next exercise we go deeper, listening to ourselves to find something that can provide a powerful motivation for practising the meditation.

exercise 12 – heart-wish

> *Once again prepare to meditate, and then tune in and listen to your heart as you did in Exercise 11. Now, patiently and receptively, open to whatever response comes, ask yourself this question: 'What is my deepest heart-wish for myself? What do I long for in my heart of hearts?' Don't worry about whether you think it is achievable, just tune in to that deep wish and let it express itself. It may come in words, but it may also express itself in images or in some other way.*

> *When it feels as if you have your answer, listen to your heart again and ask yourself a second question: 'What is my deepest heart-wish for others, for the world? What do I long for in my heart of hearts for them?' Again listen patiently for an answer, open to the possibility that it may not be what you expect.*

> *When you feel that both questions have been answered, or that things have gone as far as possible for now, bring the meditation to a close.*

You might find that asking one question in a session is enough. It might also take several sessions before answers emerge. The answers are definitely there; the difficulty is usually in persuading our everyday self to listen for them. Some people find the idea of asking their heart what it wants rather sentimental, so they don't really put themselves into the exercise. Others are anxious about what the answers might be, so they close themselves to them. But if you persist with this exercise in a spirit of openness, answers to both questions will come sooner or later.

These answers are a gift. Knowing what you want on a deep level, for yourself and others, makes a difference to your whole life. You can begin to align yourself with those deep heart-wishes, to live from them more and more. They can also provide a powerful motivation for your loving-kindness meditation. In the first stage you can wish yourself well, based on your heart-wish for yourself, and in the later stages you can tune in to your heart-wish for others to fuel your well-wishing for them.

Two questions often arise in relation to this. The first is, 'How do I know that what came up in the exercise is genuine? How can I trust it?' There will usually be a sense of rightness, of something that you have wanted all along, perhaps all your life. There may be deep emotion associated with it, or just a deep sense of knowing. The heart-wish always seems to be for something positive and beneficial, so if you found that yours wasn't, see if you can find a positive wish underlying what you came up with. For instance, someone I know came up with a desire to be in control of everyone and everything. The question then was, 'Why do you want to be in control in that way? What is the benefit for you in that?'

The question of trusting your heart-wish does raise the issue of how you trust anything in life. Buddhism traditionally says that you can have faith in something based on your reason, your intuition, and your experience. The heart-wish is a deep intuitive knowing, which you can then test against your reason and your experience of life.

The second question is usually phrased along the lines of: 'My heart-wish is all very fine, but I can't see how it could ever come about in practice. So isn't being in touch with it just going to be a source of pain and frustration for me?' For instance, you may find that your heart-wish for others is that they might all live in peace. Following the world news, with all the fighting, natural disasters, terrorism, and so forth, it may seem futile to have such a wish. Yet the fact is that it is also very painful *not* being in touch with your heart-wish. What we most deeply want and long for continues to exert an influence on us even if we hide it away and try never to think about it. In fact, most of our feelings of existential unease and frustration come from the fact that we are not in touch with, not living from, that deep place within ourselves. Life feels more satisfying when we are taking steps in the direction of our deepest wishes, however far there may be to go, however impossible it might seem that they could ever come about. So being in touch with your heart-wish, although it may at times be painful, is much more fulfilling than keeping it locked away and living on the surface of yourself.

Any time when you are doing loving-kindness meditation and find yourself getting lost in distractions, it is good to come back to your heart in this way. You can spend a few moments gazing into the distance (if you are in an enclosed space, imagine looking through the walls) to regain a sense of spaciousness so that the thoughts are not crowding in so much. Then focus on your heart and its deepest longing. This puts your distractions in perspective, widens your awareness, and helps you to contact what is really important and fulfilling for you.

This chapter has given you some tools for tapping into your core feelings, from which loving-kindness can flow naturally. In the next chapter we shall add in another vital ingredient to support the meditation.

7

empathy

In the previous chapter we looked at ways of connecting with your heart and its deepest wishes. For the meditation to really take off after the first stage, you need an open heart, but also a strong sense of the people you're meditating on. This sense of the reality of another person brings out your natural heart response. So in this chapter we'll explore ways of feeling strongly in contact with the people in the different stages of the practice. There are two aspects to this: finding ways of tuning in to the person, then getting a sense of what it would be like to be in their shoes.

making the person vivid
If I have little emotional response to someone during the meditation, it's often because I haven't produced a very strong sense of them – their presence, their reality. It is hard to feel much for a distant grey blob! To begin working on this, let's explore how you become aware of another person.

exercise 13 – noticing how you think of other people

Spend a few minutes calling different people to mind. Don't try to make them especially clear for yourself. Just be aware of what usually happens when you think 'I must call X this afternoon,' or 'I haven't seen Y for months.' Notice what faculties you use. Do you see them in your mind's eye? Do you hear the sound of their voice? Do you have some sense of their presence? Do you just think of their name? Is it some combination – perhaps variable, depending on who you are thinking of – of several of these? Or is it none of the above?

This exercise should give you a sense how you bring someone to mind. People differ greatly in the faculties they use in this way. You may use any of the five senses, concepts, or a kind of intuitive sixth-sense feeling, singly or in combination. Thankfully there isn't a 'right' way to do it. In calling people to mind you probably used one or more of these:

A sense of their presence

Their voice

A mental picture of them

Characteristic mannerisms

Things or places associated with them

Their name

Being aware of what you naturally do to call someone to mind can help you play to your strengths when thinking of people in the meditation. But this list can also help you widen out and use ways you might not have thought of. The list isn't exhaustive; you can come up with other methods to help you gain a vivid sense of someone.

Although it's helpful to make the people in your meditation as clear for you as possible, you shouldn't expect too much of yourself. All you need is enough of an internal connection with the person to enable you to develop a feeling of care and well-wishing for them. So please don't be perfectionist about it. Sometimes people assume that they should be able to see their friend in their mind's eye as clearly as if that person were standing in front of them. That can sometimes happen, but your image of your friend may often be very blurry or you might not see them at all. That's OK. For the meditation to be effective, all you need is to feel a sense of emotional connection with the person you are focusing on.

bringing the person alive
Particularly in the third and fourth stages, even a clear mental image of the person you are meditating on may not be enough to produce feelings of friendliness and well-wishing within you. You need to bring the person really alive for yourself, otherwise your heart won't respond. Here are four suggestions to help you feel more of a heart connection.

Imagine the person living their life.

Appreciate their qualities.

Recall times when they have been kind or helpful to you, or when you have shared adventures, or enjoyable or difficult times that brought you together.

Call to mind your common humanity.

You can use these in the second, third, and fourth stages, though some will work better than others with certain kinds of people. (For instance, you may not have any helpful memories of times shared with the neutral person.) Let's look at each of these in more detail.

imagine the person living their life
One of the most extraordinary abilities we have as human beings is the power of empathy. My dictionary defines this as 'the power of mentally identifying oneself with (and so fully comprehending) a person or object of contemplation'. In other words, we can put ourselves in someone else's shoes, and gain an imaginative sense of what it is like to be them, living their life. When we do this we are more able to 'fully comprehend' them and our sympathy for them increases.

When our heart is closed to someone, it is usually because we are resolutely seeing things from our own perspective and not from theirs. From that rather rigid perspective we tend to think, 'Why can't they be more like me?' We might not literally use that phrase to ourselves, but if we look at our emotional stance, that question often sums it up. Through empathy we break down this fixed position. We walk round to the other side and enter the other person's world. We become aware of their background, where they live, who they live with, the stresses and strains that they are under, their hopes and fears.

This practice of empathizing with whoever you are meditating on helps in two ways. It enables you to understand them better – and we are usually much more sympathetic to people when we understand why they act the way they do. It also breaks down the sense of distance between you and them. I really like this quote from Martin Luther King: 'Pity is feeling sorry for someone; empathy is feeling sorry with someone.' Through empathy you stand shoulder-to-shoulder with another person and share their joy and sadness. When you do this, loving-kindness and well-wishing are never far away.

Naturally, you will find it easiest to empathize with your friend, as you are likely to know most about them and find putting yourself in their shoes most congenial. With the neutral person you probably have much less to go on. You might not know much about their lives. They might be your office reception-ist or an assistant at your child's nursery. Don't let your lack of knowledge put you off. Fill out their life using your imagination. Start by imagining them do-ing their job, but then feel free to create fiction, guess-ing at where they live and how they spend time outside work. The more you make them a rounded character, the easier it will be to feel for them.

You may baulk at the idea of empathizing with some-one you find difficult, but give it your best shot. It might help you gain a deeper sense of *why* they are so tetchy, selfish, or thoughtless. According to Buddhism, everything arises in dependence upon conditions. Through empathizing, you might better understand the conditions that have caused this person's foul behaviour. You might also begin to notice, as you identify with them and their lives, that they are not all bad. Perhaps they are kind to their parents or children. They have friends, maybe people who love them. When we struggle with someone, we often become a bit fixated on some particular behaviour, or on how they treat us, and we lose sight of the bigger picture. Empathy can help us to find a new perspective from which it is easier to wish this person well.

I think of empathy as a kind of magic key to this meditation. The only thing to beware of is that you don't just spend the meditation running movies in your head about the lives of these other people, or playing Sherlock Holmes trying to pick up clues about aspects of their lives you don't know about. Imagine what it must be like to be them, in their particular circumstances, and then allow your heart to respond. Empathy is a key to the gateway of loving-kindness; make sure you use it to go through that gateway. Don't get so fascinated by your imagination that you no longer focus on a feeling of friendliness and well-wishing. That is what will have a transformative effect on your heart and mind. It will also transform your relationships with other people.

appreciate their qualities

Appreciation and loving-kindness are closely linked. You'll notice that when you are close to someone you find it easy to appreciate them. On the other hand you will find it hard to recognize good qualities in someone you really don't like. You might deny they have any at all, and hearing others praising them might make you feel a bit sick. Because of this close link, appreciation is a good way towards a more friendly feeling for someone.

Sometimes, because we don't appreciate ourselves enough, we feel hungry to be given appreciation. This makes it harder to express appreciation for others, even inwardly. We can feel like a starving person forced to help distribute food to others. But I have found over the years that through appreciating other people I have miraculously started appreciating myself more. And in the first stage of the meditation, we are learning to be on better terms with ourselves, so we are not left out.

In itself, when it doesn't make you feel deprived, focusing on appreciation is very inspiring and enjoyable. The more you do it, the more you see to appreciate. You recognize how remarkable human beings are, and how many qualities they have that you had hitherto taken for granted.

Again, you are likely to find it easiest to appreciate your friend's qualities. You probably know them well, so you have plenty of experience of them. And you often make friends with someone because they have qualities that you like or admire. If nothing else, they have very good taste in friends! The neutral person may be more of a challenge. It is interesting to look at the situation in which the person you have chosen as neutral is someone you know quite well. It may be that the qualities that they have are ones you don't value, or which you tend not to notice. Your office receptionist may be steady and reliable, courteous and helpful, but you might take all that for granted. Or you might not know much about your neutral person, the nursery assistant, say. You might never have spoken to them. But if you reflect for a moment, you know that they have some feeling for children and some sense of playfulness.

With the person you find difficult, you might have to overcome resistance. Your appreciation might at best be a grudging one. In that case, it can be helpful to appeal to your own sense of integrity. It is painful to refuse to give someone their due just because you don't like them.

recall the good times
Recall times when they have been kind or helpful to you, or when you have shared adventures, or enjoyable or difficult times that brought you together

This option isn't usually available to you in the third stage. With a friend it can work very well. By remembering a time when you were feeling particularly close, you can rekindle the strong positive feelings you had for them at that time. In the fourth stage, you might never have shared any close times with your difficult person, although you may be able to recall better days, when they were in a good mood, relatively sociable, and things were easier. Sometimes the person you are now having problems with is someone you used to feel very friendly towards, in which case recollecting old times can be good – though you will have to work with the bitter-sweet feeling of re-living a closeness that is no longer present.

Using memories in this way can be very helpful. As with empathy, just remember to let the memories be a catalyst for feelings of kindness and well-wishing. Time lost in reminiscing may be very pleasant, but it isn't meditation.

call to mind your common humanity
This involves a particular kind of empathy. When discussing this earlier, I focused on feeling what someone's life was like in their particular circumstances. This time, you concentrate on recognizing your common ground with another human being. When you put yourself in their shoes, you feel how they are breathing at this moment, just like you. They are trying to be happy, in their own way, just as you are. If you take this to an even deeper existential level, they are getting older day by day, just like you. And one day they are going to die, just as you are.

Reflecting in this way, you can tap into deep feelings of solidarity with other human beings, regardless of gender, race, politics, religious affiliation, sexual orientation, and social and financial status, or anything else. It might not be easy to connect with this at first, but if you manage to do so you will find a deep kind of well-wishing that comes out of an awareness of our shared precious, fragile human life.

This reflection works with both a friend and a neutral person, and can often dissolve away the barriers between you and the person in the fourth stage. You can also carry it over into the final stage when you expand your feeling of friendliness around the world. It can even give you a strong sense of connection with animals and other forms of life, all living, breathing creatures, who need food and shelter as you do, and who in perhaps less complex ways are trying to find happiness and avoid suffering.

It can be particularly helpful to reflect on the fact that, just as you hold yourself dear, so do all other living beings. In that sense, we are each at the centre of our own world. Feeling this, you can wish others happiness and fulfilment, just as you wish it for yourself.

Using one or more of these four methods will enhance the power of your meditation, allowing you to open yourself to others much more deeply than is possible through simply calling them to mind.

8

important distinctions

Although we all have some experience of loving-kindness, we also have experiences that can be confused with it. For the meditation to be fully effective we need to be able to distinguish the genuine article. In this chapter we'll refine the meditation by making two crucial distinctions. We'll look first at the difference between loving-kindness and what are known as its 'near enemies', and then at the difference between feelings and volitions. Being clear about these will help you to meditate more deeply, as you'll have a clearer sense of what you are trying to focus on in your practice.

'near enemies' of loving-kindness
In clarifying what loving-kindness is, Buddhism uses the helpful idea of 'near and far enemies'. To understand these, let's draw on our experience of life for a minute, and look at ways in which we've been treated over the years. What Buddhism calls the 'far enemy' of loving-kindness is its complete opposite. Sadly, we have all experienced being on the receiving end of

this from time to time. Someone has acted towards us with antagonism, even hatred or cruelty. They might have felt a personal animosity towards us as individuals, or perhaps they were just having a bad day or a bad decade, and we happened to walk into their firing line. Whichever it was, none of us has any difficulty in deciding that how we were treated was not an expression of loving-kindness.

So the far enemy, antagonism, or even hatred, is obvious enough. But if we look at our life experience we see times when someone acted towards us in ways that appeared to be motivated by loving-kindness but which turned out not to be. These are what Buddhism calls the 'near enemies' of loving-kindness. Let's look at a couple of examples, so that we can learn to tell the fool's gold from the real, precious metal.

First, you may well have experienced someone being full of kind words and protestations of friendship, but when you really needed help they didn't rally round. Maybe they had their reasons, but somehow you couldn't help feeling that there was a discrepancy between their words and their actions. This often arises out of a kind of sentimentality. People like the idea of themselves as kind and helpful, and they often are well thought of by others for their caring speech. I don't want to dismiss people who are like this. Given a choice between being faced with someone acting from the far enemy or the near enemy of loving-kindness, most of us would take the near enemy any day. Let's give these people the benefit of the doubt, and say that their loving-kindness hasn't gone very deep yet. Genuine, deep loving-kindness, by its nature, moves you into action. If a friend is in trouble and you really care about them for themselves, you will move heaven and earth, or at least get in a car or on the next train, to make sure that they are OK.

Secondly comes attachment, or conditional love. Someone might have told you how much they cared about you, how much they loved you perhaps. But when you stopped playing the role in their life that they needed you for, their apparent friendship and love vanished like thawing snow. You realize, at least with hindsight, that they loved you not for you but for themselves. You made them feel good, or secure, and when you no longer had that effect on them, or they no longer needed that security, or when you moved off the pedestal on which they wanted you to stand, their love and friendship suddenly turned into indifference, upset, or rage. Again, you can feel the difference between this kind of attachment and genuine loving-kindness, which cares about you for your own sake.

A test of someone's friendship or love comes when you start doing something which is the opposite of what they want or is in their best interests. You might have a good friend who lives close by. Then you are offered a better job, or a place at college, in another part of the country. How does your friend respond when you tell them? Of course they are sad at the prospect of seeing less of you, but if they have real loving-kindness for you, they will not be dominated by their own feelings. If they believe your new job or college course will make you happy, they will put aside their sadness and encourage you to go for it.

Looking at these two near enemies can help us to home in more precisely on what true loving-kindness is like. Although we might be confused by them for a while, there is a big difference between being on the receiving end of sentimentality or attachment and genuine loving-kindness. Real loving-kindness is altruistic, which is a rather cold word for the fact that it is open-hearted and loving. It is the kind of feeling that naturally expresses itself in loving actions. It isn't based on selfish concerns but on genuine care, appreciation, and concern. Your heart really goes out to other people, and as a result you are happy yourself.

Once, as a child, when I was being a real nuisance, my mother said to me, 'I'll always love you, but sometimes I dislike you intensely.' It was an important distinction, and one that is vital in understanding true loving-kindness. The feeling we are looking for in this meditation goes beyond likes and dislikes. In the practice we include all kinds of people: some we like, some we dislike, and some we feel indifferent towards. Just as my mother still loved me (bless her) even when I did things she really disliked, so we are looking for a deep loving-kindness that wishes people well regardless of whether they do what we want, and regardless of whether they bring us pleasure or pain.

Don't be concerned if you recognize that a lot of what you had been thinking was loving-kindness is actually sentimentality or attachment. As human beings we experience a mixture of feelings, and it is unrealistic to expect the meditation to be 100% right. It is natural to feel attachment to our friends and loved ones. To start with, our positive feelings for people we feel neutral or bad about may be more like pious hopes than anything very deep. Don't make a problem out of it. Just acknowledge the whole rich mix of your feelings and focus on empathizing with other people. The more you see life from their point of view, the more you will wish them well for themselves, and the near enemies of loving-kindness will gradually drop away.

distinguishing feelings from volitions

For the meditation to go well, we need to make another important distinction: that between *feelings* and *volitions*. At its basic level, a feeling is just the aspect of any experience that is pleasant, unpleasant, or neutral. In the practice we aim to be aware of these feelings but not driven by them. So in the fifth and final stage we do our best to develop loving-kindness equally for a friend (with whom we usually associate pleasant feelings), a person we feel neutral about, and someone we have difficulties with (so that when we think of them we often experience unpleasant feelings). Regardless of these feelings, we develop a volition – an intention by which we consciously lead our energy in a particular direction – to wish all three people well.

Feeling is automatic and, in a sense, passive. Whenever you have a perception of any kind, from the smell of a rose to the sight of a concrete slab, that experience is always accompanied by a feeling tone.

Volition is active; it is your response as an aware human being to the circumstances in which you find yourself. According to the Buddhist view, it is through these intentional actions that you mould your consciousness; they are what determine who you will become, moment by moment.

We very often live our lives on autopilot. If something has a pleasant feeling associated with it, we make a beeline for it; if it feels unpleasant, we swerve to avoid it, or move aggressively against it. If it feels neutral, we ignore it, blanking it out. In this way we can be led through life by the pleasant and the unpleasant. Where do these feelings associated with our experience come from? Essentially, when faced with a new experience our mind compares it to things we have faced in the past. If that past experience turned out well, then we experience a feeling of pleasure when something similar comes into view. If the new experience is connected with something painful, scary, or threatening from before, it will come gift-wrapped in an unpleasant feeling tone. I have liked dogs (except poodles) ever since I was a child, and whenever I see one I have a feeling of pleasure. Then a couple of years ago, while out running, I was bitten by a terrier (admittedly a rather small one). For some weeks after that incident, I noticed that the feeling when I came upon a dog was much less positive, and tinged with unpleasant feelings.

From all this we can see that if we allow ourselves to be dominated by the feeling tones associated with life around us, we shall tend to keep reproducing past behaviour patterns in a not very conscious way – unless

life happens to throw up some very different experience, like when I was bitten. Do you want to endlessly
repeat your old behaviour patterns? If you don't,
then what you need to do is create a gap of awareness
before you respond to pleasant or unpleasant feelings. In that gap, rather than carrying on in your old,
habitual way, you can put your energy into a new,
more creative behaviour – one that helps you to become a more creative and loving person. That choice
is a volition – and through creating positive volitions,
you can radically change your responses to people, to
life, to everything. That is what this meditation practice is all about, enabling you to be no longer at the
mercy of your feelings, and to become increasingly
loving and equanimous.

I have sometimes met people who practise this meditation in a kind of 'feel-good' way. If I ask them how
they do the second stage, they say something like,
'Well, I imagine myself with my good friend somewhere really beautiful – maybe lying on a beach in a
tropical paradise. I really get into the sunshine and
the lapping of the waves, and how much we're both
enjoying it. And being there with them feels really
special, and I savour how good I feel.' This is all fine,
as a warm-up. Using your imagination can be really
helpful, and imagining yourself with your friend enjoying something together can be good. But if it stops
there, then all you've done is create a lot of pleasant
feelings, and, as we've seen, that will not produce any
long-term results in terms of opening your heart.
While it may be pleasant and relaxing, it may also
encourage you to live a life lost in daydreams.

So once you have set up the conditions – and by all means take your friend off to a tropical beach in your imagination if it helps you to feel relaxed and aware of them – it is now time to do some life-changing, heart-opening work by producing a deep wish for your friend's happiness and well-being. However you do it, the aim is to become deeply caring about their welfare, just as you care about your own.

This strong volition is something that you hold to, even in the face of unpleasant feelings. A fire-fighter summoned from bed to an emergency will experience pleasant feelings associated with a warm duvet and sleep, and unpleasant feelings at the thought of suddenly getting up and rushing half-awake into the night. But their volitions – their deep wish to do their job and perhaps save lives – will overcome those temporary feelings. It's the same with a mother woken in the middle of the night by a hungry baby.

If you think about it, all the really fine, loving, heroic people that you know or have heard about all base their lives on something much deeper than superficial feelings of pleasure and discomfort. None of them follow the line of least resistance through life. They all burn with a passionate care about people and a desire to live out their deeply-held beliefs. They produce powerful volitions that override concerns about comfort and discomfort, and act in ways that affect people's lives positively.

Love is a choice, an action. It starts with choosing to act in loving ways, and eventually becomes a natural expression of who we are.

9

troubleshooting

Now that we are almost halfway through the book, and you hopefully have some experience of the meditation, this might be a good time to look at some of the problems that can arise and how to address them. We'll look first at some tendencies that often create difficulties for people, and how to counteract them. Then I'll give you a checklist of questions you can ask yourself when you feel things aren't going well.

turn towards your experience

In my early days of practising this meditation, I would often sit down, contact uncomfortable feelings – such as hatred, jealousy, or a kind of blank, grey boredom – decide I shouldn't be feeling like that, push them away, and try to feel something else. This strategy rarely worked. When it did, the positive feeling I developed was never very deep or stable. A basic guideline for meditation is always to turn towards your experience – whatever it is, and especially if it doesn't fit with your idea of how it should be. These days, if I find such feelings, I make sure I fully acknowledge them. Through contacting the energy within them, I can often lead the meditation into more positive ways of expressing itself.

It can be helpful to look at your motivation for ignoring difficult feelings and hurrying to something more positive. There are several possibilities, including (1) wanting to shut out difficult emotions because they are taken as confirmation of a low self-image, (2) an idea that it's not 'spiritual' or 'Buddhist' to experience these things, or (3) you don't know what to do about them.

When you find yourself experiencing difficult feelings, you need to sit with them as you would another person. If I was trying to persuade you to change some behaviour, I wouldn't get very far if you felt I wanted you to change because I found you unpleasant or inconvenient. I would have a much better chance of having an influence if you felt I was genuinely interested in you and your welfare. The same applies in our relationship with ourselves. Some more superficial moods and feelings can be dispelled by an act of will. But you will only gain leverage over more intractable negative feelings through deep acknowledgement and holding them in kindly awareness.

True, you can sometimes decide to set aside unhelpful feelings and set to work to cultivate something more akin to loving-kindness, but you should be wary of leaping over your current feelings into some supposedly more ideal state of mind.

hold expectations lightly

When I teach new people loving-kindness meditation, they sometimes have surprisingly good experiences. This is because the meditation was completely fresh for them, and they went into it without expectations. However, as people keep practising, they often build up very definite expectations based on their experience of meditation so far. This is just human nature, but it is good to hold these expectations lightly, so that you stay open to the moment. Some people find the practice hard to start with. This conditions them to expect it will always be like that, which can create a bit of a self-fulfilling prophecy.

Other people have an excellent early experience. They find themselves feeling very loving, expansive, and concentrated, and then expect the meditation to work like that every time. However, because everything changes, they are setting themselves up for disappointment. I sometimes liken this to a young brother and sister who like to explore the hillside near their village. One day they come to a cliff of very smooth, bare rock. They sit down, and one of them happens to lean on a boulder, which causes something extraordinary to happen. Part of the rock face begins to open, like a gateway. Amazed, the children decide to go in. Inside they find all kinds of wonders; it's a fairy kingdom, full of riches. The inhabitants allow them to explore for a while, and then return them to the hillside. The rock gateway swings smoothly shut. The children are entranced by what they have found. The next day, trembling with excitement, they hurry back to the cliff face and push against the boulder. Nothing happens. The cliff face frowns down at them, impassive.

Although you have set up all the conditions for meditation, you can never be sure you will take off into higher or deeper realms of experience. One day you might have a deep experience, and the next day you might feel you are doing exactly the same thing, but with no obvious result. It takes a while to realize that meditation is about deep forces within the heart and mind that are not fully under our control. All that you, the conscious subject, can contribute is to faithfully do your best. The children can only keep coming back to the cliff, push boulders, and patiently wait. It is painful when meditation isn't as fulfilling as you know it can be. Rather than endure that pain, you might be tempted to give up. That would be a tragedy. If the children are faithful, and trust their knowledge that there *is* a magical realm within the rock, then one day they will find the gateway open again. If they keep faithfully turning up, they will eventually find they have free and permanent access to that magical world.

unhook emotions from their context
When you focus on your emotions in this meditation, you will over time experience the full gamut of feelings, from joy and bliss to rage and craving. When difficult feelings do come up, it is helpful to think of them as raw material. After all, there is often much energy tied up in emotions like anger, craving, or jealousy. It is a question of changing your attitude to them and seeing them as an opportunity rather than something that gets in the way.

Unhooking is an effective way to work with strong negative feelings such as anger. Let's suppose that someone has wronged you and you are furious with them. The first step is to acknowledge the situation. You might not like it, but there you are, pawing the ground, with steam coming out of your nostrils. As you do this, a whole story is going through your head about what this person has done. Unhooking involves putting down, or letting go, of this story. You cease to concern yourself with the object – the person or situation that has got you mad. You even let go of thinking about the subject – you, and what has been done to you. Rather than focus on the cause of your anger, you simply concentrate on the state of anger itself.

Doing this might not feel very comfortable, as it often causes the physical sensations of anger to intensify. But then you unhook even the idea that what you are experiencing is anger. Just feel the pure sensations: the heat in your body, the contracted muscles, and so on. If you keep doing this, you may well find that what you are now experiencing is simply a great deal of energy coursing through your body. This energy is quite free-flowing (because it is not fixated on the person who 'made you angry' any more). With practice, you'll be able to experience it fully and allow it to flow more constructively.

allow energy releases
As your practice deepens, emotional tensions start to loosen up. These releases can come in different ways. You might find yourself in fits of laughter in the meditation, or in floods of tears. Events from the past may

surface. Your body might shake involuntarily, or you might feel energy movements in your spine. These are all good signs, but you might feel uneasy if you don't understand what is happening. Some people have a lot of this kind of experience; others almost none. The best approach is to aim for a middle way: don't hold them at bay, but don't go chasing after them or trying to prolong them either.

be content with the process of meditation

When people start practising this meditation, a common tendency is to expect too much too soon. We don't often live very close to our feelings, so we only notice big, loud emotions. We expect to have feelings of loving-kindness as strong as our peak moments, or our most powerful times of feeling in love. As a result, we ignore the subtler, quieter, unassuming feelings of kindness and love that we are actually experiencing. Be aware of any tendency to do this meditation like an impatient gardener, clomping around in heavy boots, stomping on shoots and seedlings in frustration that you can't see any mature plants.

Sometimes the meditation *may* feel powerful; you might even be overwhelmed with oceanic feelings of love and kindness. But there will often be just a sense of some emotional movement, so that when you get up afterwards, your heart feels a little lighter and more open than when you sat down. That is a sign that you are on the right track. We talk about meditation as a 'practice' – and practice makes perfect.

a troubleshooting checklist

In the course of the next six chapters, we'll go through the five stages of the meditation individually, looking at particular issues that can arise in each one. Before we launch into that, this would be a good place to give you some troubleshooting tools. Here are some questions that it is helpful to ask when you feel the meditation isn't happening for you.

Am I in touch with my basic experience? Before trying to develop any kind of positive feeling, check that you are you in contact with your body. Can you feel yourself sitting on your cushion, stool, or chair? Can you feel your breath?

What am I feeling now? Come back to that without judging it. Acknowledge how you are. Honestly saying, 'I feel tired, ratty, and can't feel anything for my friend at the moment,' is sometimes the beginning of a good meditation.

Am I being perfectionist? Giving yourself a hard time because you're not 'doing it right' has nothing to do with loving-kindness. It will prevent you from relaxing and enjoying the practice. Back off. Be sensitive to yourself. Don't be judgemental about being judgemental. Let all those thoughts just come and go. Tune in to your body.

Am I making the right kind of effort? Trying to force the feeling is counter-productive. A gentle, steady effort is usually the most effective.

What do I need? If you're in contact with how you're feeling, this can often be a helpful question to ask. Sometimes you just need to sit with yourself for a while, to bear witness to what is happening in your heart-mind and in your body, before you are ready to do anything else.

Do I have a definite sense of the person I'm meditating on? If you're in touch with yourself and your feeling, and the practice is still flat, this is usually the missing factor. Can you feel them as a living, breathing person like you? Can you put yourself in their shoes?

I could make this list much more elaborate, but these six questions should usually be enough to give you a sense of what you need to do as a next step.

If you're in touch with yourself, your feeling of loving-kindness, and the person you're sending it to, then you can trust that the practice will be effective. Just be patient and keep going. Sometimes people who are new to the meditation set up all the right conditions except one: confidence that it will work. You may just need to relax and not concern yourself with when it is going to happen, or whether you are doing it right. Our hearts are amazing; we can trust them to find their way.

It is also good to bear in mind that loving-kindness isn't usually a very consistent feeling. It tends to come in waves. Even when the practice is going well and I am in touch with care and kindness, there are ebbs and flows, pulses of stronger feeling and pauses when less is happening. Rather than being concerned when the strength of my feeling is reduced, I find it helps if I listen more carefully to my heart. Instead of berating myself or feeling disappointed – which would just take me off track – I am sensitive to the first beginnings of a new wave of positive feeling. According to the Buddhist view, whatever aspect of your experience you put your energy and awareness into tends to grow. So you can sit and wait, patiently and confidently, like someone watching the eastern horizon for signs of the dawn.

10

the first stage

issues of self-esteem

There is a well-known story about a tourist who stops at a village in Ireland and asks one of the locals how to get to Dublin. The villager looks at him dubiously, and with a shake of his head replies, 'Well, if I wanted to go to Dublin, I wouldn't be starting from here.' I told this story once in a workshop to illustrate a point, and an Irish woman who was present was very upset with me, saying that I was reinforcing a stereotype of the Irish as not very bright. I was perplexed, as it had never occurred to me to think of the villager's response as stupid. (And anyway, my father's family came originally from the west of Ireland.)

I had told the story because I felt it held a truth about me and many other people I know. I have often sat down at the beginning of a loving-kindness medita-tion, explored how I was feeling, and promptly felt very despondent because it was a million miles away from love and friendliness. At that point, I often think of that story, and say to myself, 'If I wanted to develop loving-kindness, I wouldn't be starting from here.' That makes me smile, as I recognize the absurdity of trying to start from anywhere other than where I am. Wherever you are, there is always some way to get to Dublin. It may not be very quick, it may not be very direct, but, with patience and determination, you can always get there somehow. The same is true for the development of friendliness and love.

The five-stage meditation begins with ourselves, and for westerners this may not be an easy starting point. In the Asian Buddhist tradition, it is considered a simple place to start, as it is assumed that we naturally all care for ourselves and wish ourselves well. However, for westerners this issue is often not as straightforward. We needn't go into the reasons here, but many people in our society are not on good terms with themselves, and suffer from anything from low self-esteem to self-hatred.

In teaching this meditation, I have seen again and again that, in the first stage, even straightforward suggestions can prove to be quite complex for people. For instance, I might suggest that in the first stage you could sometimes use the phrase 'May I be well'. Someone who generally feels 'not OK' about themselves might take this to mean 'May I get better,' as if there were something the matter with them, when in fact it may just mean wishing that they continue to be well in the future.

So we need to be aware that this first stage of the meditation might bring up some difficult issues. It might take some courage to venture into it. For some of us, saying things like, 'May I be really happy and free,' means venturing into the dragon's den of our lack of self-worth and poking it with a stick. But this dragon (and his ugly brothers and sisters like self-loathing and negative self-criticism) has been squatting on our lives far too long. This meditation, practised regularly over time, can rid our inner landscape of them once and for all. Doing this will also be a gift to others, as we shall be able to give them a sense, through who we are, that it is possible, good even, to care for yourself and to love yourself in a non-egotistic, unselfish way.

Of course, many westerners are on good terms with themselves, and none of the above applies to them. If you are one of these, that's great: you can enjoy doing this first stage of the meditation. Please be sympathetic and send some loving-kindness to those of us who find it harder going. You can skip parts of this chapter, or read them with an eye out for tips for helping any people you meet who struggle with their self-esteem.

It is important to recognize that we keep up our lack of appreciation for ourselves by focusing on aspects of our behaviour that reinforce our negative self-image and ignoring or devaluing those that don't. We often display more goodness in our lives than we realize, but we take it for granted and focus on what isn't right. In personality terms, we often do the equivalent of a supermodel, who millions agree is beautiful but who might say, 'I think my mouth looks ugly.' We often do the same thing with ourselves. We totally ignore or take for granted quite obvious good qualities, and focus on some minor blemish in our personality or behaviour.

Even when we do notice something good about ourselves, or are complimented by others, we often find ways of dismissing it. Sometimes we seem determined not to give ourselves any credit, or acknowledge any good qualities in ourselves at all. If you've really decided not to feel good about yourself, here is *A Brief Guide to Avoiding Accepting Kindness and Appreciation*. It doesn't matter whether the positive appreciation is coming from someone else or (even worse!) from yourself; there are a number of ways of completely defusing it.

1. Start with stout denial.
'You did that really well.'
'No I didn't, I made a complete hash of it.'

'That was very generous.'
'No, it was the least I could get away with.'

'Wow, a degree in astrophysics, you're really intelligent.' 'No, I'm not very bright; I'm useless at crosswords.'

2. If you can't deny the facts, deny responsibility or any positive motivation.
'You did that really well.'
'Yes, but I just got lucky.'

'You were very patient.'
'Yes, but I felt like throttling him.'

'That was very generous.'
'Yes, but I only did it because I felt guilty.'

(Notice that these all begin with 'Yes, but …'. You should practise this phrase; it will come in very useful.)

3. If you are forced to acknowledge something posi-tive, deny that you are in any way special or above average.
Useful phrases here are, 'Well everyone does that, don't they?' or, 'Anyone in my position would have done the same.' (The latter is often used by people under headlines like 'Heroine Rescues Sleeping Fam-ily from Flames' or 'Man Dives Into Icy River to Res-cue Neighbour's Son's Pet Hamster' when it is clear that a lot of people in their position wouldn't have dreamed of doing the same.)

4. If you are finally cornered into acknowledging that you have positive qualities, bring out the killer sen-tence that negates them all:
'Yes, but if people knew what I was *really* like.…'

I've caricatured these to make them easier to recog-nize, and also because if you are like this, one of the first things to do is to lighten up around it, and not take the whole issue so seriously.

It is good to look out for all four of these in medita-tion. In the first stage, you might notice yourself denying that you ever do anything good or have any positive qualities. (This is strategy number 1 above.) Through meditation, you will become more aware and begin to notice various times when you are gen-erous, caring, and so forth. At that point you will need to watch out for a tendency to undercut them in one way or another (number 2). As you keep practising, you will find yourself on better terms with yourself, at which point, often when the delicate plant of self-esteem is just poking above the ground, you may decide you are getting 'above yourself' and start questioning how you are in any way special (number 3). Finally, when it is becoming obvious that you do have a lot to offer as a person, you may run up against an ill-defined sense that there is something deeply the matter with you (number 4) – though when you try to explain what is so awful, it usually doesn't amount to very much.

That phrase, 'if people knew what I was *really* like,' is funny really. The fact is that *we* often don't know what we're really like. We live on the surface of ourselves, too scared of what we might find if we go and take a good look. We often live in a world of fears about what we *might* be like rather than deep first-hand knowledge. Meditation is an excellent way of discovering what we are like. As we spend time sitting very directly with our experience, we come to know ourselves very well. Yes, we discover things we don't like or find difficult which we have to turn towards and engage with in a kindly way. But we also discover deep resources of love, kindness, and care that we barely knew existed.

The following exercise is an effective way of working with these issues, by giving us a new perspective from which to view ourselves. Within it, we see ourselves through the eyes of a friend, relative, or mentor who is perhaps more objective about us than we can be.

exercise 14 – a good friend's perspective

Next time you do the meditation, in the first stage put yourself in the shoes of someone who you know cares about you. See yourself through their eyes. Have a sense of how they value you and wish your well. Then identify with yourself, and allow yourself to feel some of that same appreciation, care, and kindness for yourself.

Professional players of these defences against appreciation may find that even seeing themselves reflected in the eyes of someone who values them is not enough. They tell themselves that their friend is just taking pity on them, or that they have managed to con their friend so that they don't see their awful faults and failings. For people like this – which might be most of us on a bad day – I recommend the next exercise.

exercise 15 – seeing yourself through kindly eyes

This is very similar to the previous exercise. There you saw yourself from the viewpoint of someone you knew cared for and appreciated you – a friend, relative, or colleague. This time, do the first stage of the meditation seeing yourself through the eyes of someone very loving and compassionate. You don't have to know this person. It could be someone you've read about whose life or example you find moving or inspiring. You could even try it with someone who died centuries ago, or a fictional character. Imagine yourself in their presence, and feel their kindly awareness of you. How do they respond to you? If you find yourself 'yes, butting' or closing yourself off to them, try telling them what you are doing, why you aren't lovable, and let them respond. Allow yourself to enjoy being in their presence, soak up their warmth like sunshine.

Along with low self-esteem inevitably comes a sense that you have little to give anyone else. People who feel like this sometimes ask if it would be OK to spend all their meditation time on the first stage of the practice until they have more to offer. This can be all right for a little while, but I wouldn't recommend doing it for long. When you focus on yourself all the time, you tend to narrow your horizons, and develop a bit of a 'poverty mentality' – as if there isn't enough love to go around, and if you give it to yourself then you won't have enough to give to others. I have found that focusing on others and wishing them well can also make me feel better about myself.

In any case, all the stages of the meditation help you to be on better terms with yourself. As you work through the five stages, you are ostensibly directing feelings towards different people. But because your outer and inner worlds are related, you are also changing your relationship with yourself. If you see yourself as a collection of aspects, then there are parts of yourself that you particularly identify with, what you naturally think of as 'you'. You have aspects of yourself that you like, and are on good terms with, aspects that you take for granted, or don't have feelings about one way or the other, and aspects that you really dislike, that cause you trouble and conflict. So the stages work both on changing your relationship with others and with aspects of yourself. For example, it is a commonplace of psychology that what you dislike most in other people is often a projection of what you find unacceptable in yourself. So when you change your relationship to the difficult person, you may find at the same time that aspects of yourself that had felt difficult and intractable are softening and coming into an easier relationship with the rest of your personality.

confusing positive self-regard with egotism

In the first stage of the meditation, it is very important to be able to distinguish between unhealthy egotism and healthy self-regard. In policing ourselves for examples of the former, we can end up chronically deficient in the latter. You are special, in the sense that you are a unique individual. There never has been, and never will be, someone quite like you. You are also special in the sense that all life is special. As a unique being, your feelings and perceptions are of value. You contribute something to the world just by being here, apart from any contribution you might make by what you do.

You are not special, in the sense that you share the planet with billions of other human beings and untold numbers of other life-forms. Your needs and desires are no more important than theirs, and you are not entitled to assert your wishes without regard to them. One of the deeper lessons of this practice of loving-kindness is that we are all interconnected. When we see that, we see the unique contribution we could make, and our life becomes rich and meaningful. Egotism is an attempt to cut the subtle strings of connection to life and to assert ourselves independently of the whole. It leaves us feeling bereft and cut off from life.

Positive self-regard isn't developed at the expense of others. It doesn't come out of a feeling of poverty – that there is only so much love and appreciation to go round and we have to fight for our share. It comes from a sense of richness. We can give and receive love because it is inexhaustible. With egotism we want the spotlight turned on ourselves all the time, until others become bored and frustrated and turn away from us. With positive self-regard, we are happy for others to be in the spotlight, and happy to take our turn, to do our best, and to acknowledge the appreciation we receive. Life is a dance in which we all have our part to play.

11

the good friend

For many people, the second stage of the meditation is the easiest and most natural one of the five. Calling to mind a good friend is usually a pleasure, and it is easy to meditate when your meditation subject is an enjoyable one. But still, the second stage isn't always straightforward, and there are some questions that commonly come up.

If it feels as though this stage isn't going well, this is often because you are putting unrealistic expectations on it. You might call your friend to mind and not feel much for them. Or they might have irritated you recently, so your feeling for them might not be the amiable caring that you expected. Don't be concerned about this, or start feeling guilty about not feeling more. The first thing to do is always to turn towards and acknowledge your actual experience, whatever that is. Calling to mind a good friend is no guarantee of feeling friendliness and well-wishing. We have seen that loving-kindness isn't under our control. We can't produce it to order. All we can do is set up the conditions for it to arise.

Thinking of someone we care about is often enough to produce the conditions we need to feel loving-kindness. But if it isn't, don't worry. We know that we care about this person, and we generally wish them well. It is just a question of accessing those feelings. What we *don't* do is tell ourselves off and feel guilty that we cannot feel anything, even for our friends. There is no need to be mean to yourself in that way. You aren't a machine, churning out feelings to order; you're a human being with all kinds of subtle and complex emotional and physical processes.

One thing that can get in the way is resistance to leaving the first stage and moving on to your friend. Sometimes loving-kindness for ourselves feels like something we need very badly. We might not feel ready to turn our attention to someone else when we are still drinking it in ourselves like a thirsty plant. If this happens to you, there is no need to see things in either/or terms. Call your friend to mind, and wish them well in addition to, rather than instead of, yourself. If you are using phrases, rather than say, 'May you be well,' and so on, you can say 'May we be well.'

If you find you still aren't making a positive emotional connection with your friend, you can try some of the methods that we looked at in the chapter on empathy: remembering a time when you and your friend were really in tune, when you did feel close to them, or reflecting on their qualities, or on your shared humanity. Something that can also help is to imagine telling someone why this person is such a good friend.

If none of the above is working, then spend some time exploring what is going on. Is there something specific getting in the way of your positive feelings? Even in a good friendship there are likely to be difficult feelings sometimes: jealousy, feeling unappreciated, annoyance, for example. I remember once talking to a young schoolgirl. During our conversation she suddenly pointed to another girl playing in the distance, grimaced, and said, 'She's my best friend and I *hate* her!' If you find something in the way, acknowledge it, do your best to accept that it's there, and then see if you can put it into a wider perspective. The reality of any friendship is that people are mixed; our responses to them are also mixed. Accepting this with loving-kindness is part of what makes both friendship and this meditation work. They both require a lot of tolerance and forgiveness.

In meditation, the aim is never to sweep things under the carpet. In fact, meditation has the effect of rolling back the carpet, exposing your true feelings and allowing them to become fully conscious. This might feel uncomfortable at times, but it is a great gain. When your feelings are unacknowledged, they exert an influence over you. To some extent you are in their power, with no choice to act differently. When they become conscious, you get to know them fully, and become better able to decide whether or not to go along with them.

Of course, it may be that what is preventing you from making the connection with your friend has nothing to do with them. You could be feeling too tired to summon up the energy to meditate, or you might have something on your mind that is getting in the way.

should I stick with the same person in the meditation each time?

You can choose various friends to put in the second stage for different meditation sessions. At first, it is interesting to explore how the meditation feels when you include different kinds of people. However, there is something to be said for staying with one person for a few days, weeks, or even months. It means you don't have to expend time or energy deciding who to choose for the meditation. More than that, repeated meditation on one friend can allow you to focus more strongly, and sometimes to go deeper in the meditation. Over time, you come to know your emotional responses to this person very well, and your loving-kindness for them can become very strong. When you stay with the same person in this way, you are most likely to notice how your meditation is having a positive effect in the outside world, and that your friendship is deepening as a result of the emotional work you have been doing.

If you do decide to put the same person in the second stage regularly, then it is good to review how it is going from time to time. Ask yourself if doing so is helping you to build up momentum in the second stage. Are you being creative, and deepening your feeling for your friend? Or has it all gone a bit dead and habitual? (In which case, a change might enliven things again.) Is sticking to the same person helping you to get into the groove, or into a rut?

why do I have to limit my choices in this stage?

This stage sets the tone for the rest of the meditation, and choosing the right kind of person sets you on the right track for the further stages. While you are becoming familiar with the meditation, limiting the options helps you to find the true feeling, rather than its near enemies. But once you have been meditating for a while, you can try experimenting with widening your circle of possibilities to include people who are older or younger, people who have died, and those you are attracted to. Try to be very honest with yourself about this. If you find it doesn't help the meditation, then go back to choosing within the parameters we started with. Those recommendations about age and so on are traditional, and they are there for a reason. It is worth taking them seriously, although finally you have to trust your experience. After all, it is your heart, your mind.

These days I am pretty relaxed about who I put in the second stage, but for many years I followed the guidelines closely, and found them helpful. When I experimented with letting them go, I noticed some difficulties. For instance, if I focused on someone I was attracted to, although I would try not to get into sexual fantasy, I would notice that after the highly-charged second stage the neutral person seemed very bland and boring. Rather than experiencing their common humanity, I felt the lack of the romantic excitement that had been there in the previous stage.

So I suggest that you follow the guidelines for this stage until you have a good deal of experience, and then see for yourself what happens when you ignore them. By then, you will have gained a real taste for what loving-kindness feels like, and you will know when what you are practising is the development of something else.

12

the neutral person

And if you can't be with the one you love,
Love the one you're with.
Stephen Stills

As a hippie in the early 1970s, those lines from a song
by one of my favourite bands struck me very forcibly.
I later forgot all about them, until I had been practising loving-kindness meditation for several years.
Then one day I started thinking about how I treated
people. I had to admit there was a gulf between how I
was with my close friends and how I acted around the
rest of humanity. That felt quite natural and understandable. But then I began reflecting on how happy
it made me to treat my friends well. With at least a few
people I was reasonably kind and generous, and acting in that way made me happy. I felt good about myself. I enjoyed seeing these people that I cared about,
but I also enjoyed the 'me' that came out when they
were around. It was kind, sunny, encouraging. So
then it dawned on me: if I enjoy acting in this way
towards my close friends, why don't I widen that

feeling out? Why don't I shift my attitude and treat everyone as if they were a close friend? I knew that was an impossible ideal, but I sensed that by changing my attitude I would be able to operate more in that way, and that by doing so I'd feel happier about myself and make my corner of the world a warmer place.

This stage tends to be harder work than the previous two, since with a neutral person you have made no emotional investment, and have to start from scratch. Also you probably know less about this person than you do about your friend, so you might need to use more imagination to fill in the gaps and give yourself a sense of this person's life, their hopes and aspirations, their struggles and fears.

But, after all, there is only one of us, and we have a limited number of friends and loved ones, so most of the billions of people on this planet fall into this third category. If we could change our feelings for them, that would be fantastic. Just imagine what it would be like if, rather than feeling neutral about most people, your first response on seeing another human being was one of pleasure and happiness. It can sometimes happen. If you have been on your own and haven't seen anyone for quite a while, you might be pleased just to see someone. And certainly there are times when you are in a bit of trouble, perhaps lost in a strange place, and someone comes into view, just a neutral person, and you are really happy to see them.

I once came upon an old lady sitting still in her parked car, in an unnatural position. I examined her and could find no signs of breath or heartbeat. I felt very alone with this probably-deceased person and my acute lack of medical knowledge. Should I be trying to resuscitate her? At that moment a young woman came walking down the street towards me. It was great to see someone I could talk to. She stopped, and her first words were, 'I'm a nurse. Can I help?' Suddenly I didn't feel neutral at all about this nameless stranger. In fact I could have kissed her. (Incidentally, the old lady had just dropped a friend in a nearby café and gone to park her car. She could not be helped. 'She's lucky to go like that,' said the nurse.)

The main way into this stage is to get in touch with a sense that this person is a human being like you. You need to empathize in the way I mentioned earlier. Their life circumstances may be very different from yours – you might be a student and they might be a tax lawyer, or vice versa but in all the essentials they are the same. Like you, they were born and grew up. Like you, they get sick from time to time. Like you, they are getting older day by day. Like you, they will die (and they don't know when).

Not only are their fundamental life circumstances similar, they also have the same basic emotional responses to life. They want pleasurable things to continue, they want unpleasant experiences to stop, they don't like it when enjoyable circumstances change. This is true for all human beings: male or female, nine or ninety, mega-rich or on the street, sensible and trustworthy or criminally insane. In fact it is true of all living beings.

exercise 16 – faces in the crowd

Next time you are in a crowded place – a shopping mall, a railway station or airport, a busy street – just stop for a little while and stand as if you were waiting for someone. Watch the people walking past. Without staring, just take them in: their facial expressions, their different bodily shapes, the ways in which they walk, stand, or sit.

As you do this, you will find your mind making judgements about what you see. You are instinctively drawn to some people and averse to others. This may be based on obvious things such as their attractiveness, how healthy they look, how they are dressed, and perhaps on subtler intuitive cues. Try to let go of these preferences. Focus on what all these people have in common – that young mother with the toddler, that old man in a grey suit, that pair of youths in trainers. Try to feel the common humanity behind the smiles and frowns, the hairstyles and the wrinkles. That old man was once a toddler. Right now everyone you can see, each in their own particular way, is trying to avoid suffering and be happy. Tune in to a sense of solidarity with all these people. Whoever we are, we are all in the same boat – hearts pumping, lungs working – facing the same fundamental life issues. Allow your heart to open to all these fellow human beings.

You can also perform this exercise while travelling in busy trains or buses. It can be an absorbing, even moving, way to pass a journey.

objections to the third stage

As with all the stages, your mind will at times throw up reasons for not engaging with the meditation. In this stage, the most common objection is basically 'this is *boring*.' The neutral person is just that: neutral.

Very often, people are neutral because they don't play any very important part in our world. They don't do much for us, either literally or figuratively. In this third stage, we really have to step beyond self-concern and begin to take an interest in people for themselves. A reflection I mentioned earlier can be very useful here: these people all hold themselves dear, just as we hold ourselves dear. Each of us is a kind of sun around which everything else revolves. Everything centres on our body, which is the view-point from which we experience things. We are all valuable to ourselves, protecting our bodies from harm and ourselves from pain and unhappiness. When we see how someone else wants happiness for themselves just as we want happiness, how they are involved in that grand and frustrating project, we can often feel more for them.

I also find it helpful to remember some of my initial bored or condescending inner responses to people whom I subsequently, and humiliatingly, discovered were remarkable people. It is all too easy to write people off after a superficial acquaintance. A friend of mine tells a story that illustrates this very well. He was a company director who liked to take an interest in his workforce. One man who worked on the factory floor seemed very ordinary, and talked only about work. My friend couldn't find any way to engage with him, and eventually concluded that there wasn't much to engage with. Then one day he noticed his car had a bumper sticker about archery. So the next time they met, my friend said, 'I see you're into archery.' 'Yes,' the man replied, 'I am quite keen on it.' End of conversation. My friend thought, 'Oh well, so much for that,' and gave up. Later he was taken aside by a colleague who had overheard the exchange. 'Quite keen on archery?' he said, 'He's an Olympic gold medallist!'

To develop more of a sense of appreciation for people in this third stage, I sometimes reflect on all the anonymous people who enable me to live my life. Any meal that I eat is the product of the efforts of a network of people: farmers, lorry drivers, shop workers, and so on. And all those people are in their turn supported by networks of their own. We often take all this for granted until something, or someone, fails. But reflecting in this way, cultivating a sense of our interdependence with others, and a sense of gratitude for what they do for us, can help us to open our hearts to all these 'uninteresting' people.

13

the person you find difficult

*Darkness cannot run out darkness;
only light can do that.
Hate cannot run out hate; only love can do that.'*
Martin Luther King Jr

For most of us, most of the time, this stage is likely to be the most challenging. It is asking us to go against our natural instincts and wish someone well when we find it painful to call them to mind. As I suggested earlier, it is good to start with people you don't find too difficult, and then take on greater challenges as your reserves of loving-kindness develop. Some people prefer this stage to the previous one. With someone you find quite neutral, there is little engagement; you don't have much energy invested in your relationship with them. At least in this fourth stage there is energy. This person impinges significantly on your life and there is a definite emotional connection between you. Sometimes it is easier to take that energy and change its direction by a kind of emotional aikido, rather than trying to build up some energy in order to feel a connection with the neutral person.

It is worth noticing that, unless the person in this stage has done something terrible to you, you do wish them well to some extent. If you heard they had died, you probably wouldn't really wear your dancing shoes at their burial. Yes, you want them to act differently towards you, but on some level you recognize them as a living, breathing human being like you, and deep down you don't wish them to be unwell, unhappy, suffering, and unable to find the path to freedom. In fact you probably wish them well, happy, and free, but with some more insight into their character and behaviour.

In this stage I *can* often acknowledge that underneath the difficult feelings I still wish this person well. The issue is whether I can be big enough to open my heart to that person when they are annoying, frustrating, or upsetting me so much. Opening my heart to them would mean letting go of resentment, irritation, the desire to get even, and so on. That often isn't easy. To help myself do so, I have a question and a reflection that I find helpful.

The question is, 'Are you enjoying feeling like this?' I can get so caught up in irritation and frustration, and feel so justified in feeling that way, that I don't notice what an unpleasant frame of mind it is. All I get from it is the chance to feel superior to this other person who has been so stupid, selfish, or whatever. For that dubious pleasure I stomp around with my blood pressure rising, tense and wound up, and I don't notice the sun on the trees outside. It often seems that my response to being briefly hurt or upset by someone else is to do far worse to myself for much longer.

The reflection is that by getting angry and annoyed by some probably trivial thing that someone has said or done, I am acting in the same way that, on a larger scale, causes wars and atrocities around the world. If I get *that* upset about someone not clearing up after themselves, how would I respond if I lived in a war zone and some of my family were killed? I don't get out an AK-47 in response to someone forgetting to clean the shower, or bomb my local council for giving me a parking ticket. But the cycle of provocation, feelings of justified anger, and desire to retaliate is still the same. I may not be able to do much about the world's trouble spots, but I *can* uproot the tendencies to hatred and violence in my own heart, and ensure that, at least in my small corner of the world, I am promoting peace and understanding.

I don't introduce this question and reflection at the beginning of this stage. I call someone to mind, acknowledge my present feelings for them, try to see them as a human being in a much broader context than my current difficulty with them, look for things to appreciate, and wish them well. That often does the trick, but when it doesn't, and I still feel up in arms or stony-hearted towards them, then I start asking myself if I am enjoying feeling like that, or reflecting on how feelings like this cause so much misery.

loving-kindness and patience

What do you do when someone starts to anger or annoy you? People often try to stay calm, perhaps taking a deep breath or two, maybe even counting to ten. This kind of forced patience is OK as an emergency measure, but through meditation we can find much more effective ways to respond in these situations. The secret (again) is empathy. If you can learn in meditation to put yourself in the position of someone who is annoying you, then when you are under pressure, when someone is being unreasonable or unpleasant, you will have new ways of responding. Rather than just falling into your own feelings of hurt and upset, you will be able to ask yourself, 'Why are they acting like this?'

The American business guru Stephen Covey tells a story about being on a subway. The people in the car are all sitting quietly. Then a man gets on with his children. The children just run riot down the car and disturb everybody. The father takes no notice. Covey, who is irritated, very politely says, 'Are you aware that your children are disturbing a lot of people?' The man, who seems lost in a reverie, rouses himself and replies, 'Oh, I'm sorry, I suppose I ought to do something about them, but their mother died in hospital about an hour ago. I just don't know how to handle it and I guess they don't either.'

At that point, Covey's whole attitude changes completely. He no longer has to practise being patient with these people. He suddenly understands why they are acting in this way. In a few seconds he goes from being angry and frustrated to feeling concern and wishing to help. Understanding is what really enables you to be patient. In fact, when you understand a situation, you often do not realize you are practising patience because you quite naturally respond calmly.

In the fourth stage, if you are not finding it easy to overcome your initial feelings of dislike or animosity, you can always work to empathize. For instance, if someone is a bit short-tempered or seems to be trying to railroad you into doing something, through empathizing you might realize that this is their response to feeling anxious and under pressure. That is understandable, and you can allow some sympathy for them to soften your stance.

Sometimes when I try to empathize I cannot see anything in the immediate circumstances that caused someone to act as they did. But later, if I hear more of the story of their life, my attitude completely changes. Given their conditions, their behaviour is a natural response. It is their attempt at happiness. Understanding really transforms everything.

Most of the time, it is enough to put yourself in the other person's situation and get a sense of what is driving their behaviour on an everyday level. But when you empathize with another human being, you sooner or later become aware of something deeper. You bump into a kind of existential unsatisfactoriness that drives them – that drives all of us. It is this fundamental sense of unsatisfactoriness – that can never be fully satisfied, hard as we try to make our lives work – that Buddhism aims to eradicate. Finally, it is this deep feeling of unsatisfactoriness that drives people to act in ways that you find difficult. When people act in unhelpful ways, there is always some sense of unsatisfactoriness there that is digging into them and provoking that response. Their action is an attempt to get out of that pain. When you go deeply into yourself in meditation, you will find that it is that same deep sense of frustration, unsatisfactoriness, of something unfulfilled, that is driving your negative responses as well.

In our different ways, we all experience life as unsatisfactory, and we are all striving for happiness. When, through empathy, your sense of the unsatisfactoriness of mundane life resonates with that of another human being, it gives you a deep sense of human solidarity. That fellow-feeling makes you patient and tolerant with people. You still might not agree with them; you might even have to stand up and oppose them, but that empathy, that resonance of shared unsatisfactoriness, will link you on a deeper level.

Even if you fail to understand someone, you can still be sure that there must somewhere be an explanation for their actions. Just that belief is often sufficient to make you more patient with them.

A few years ago, I was teaching this meditation to a group of friends who knew a lot of people in common. One person mentioned that in the fourth stage, she had chosen one particular person, and a few of the others in the group murmured in sympathy. She said that this man was so unpleasant that he had even been obstructive when she needed to take her sick child to the hospital. So we started talking about this man, and after a while we started feeling our way into his position. We got to a point where we thought, 'Well, it must be really painful to live in a world that is so isolated, so cut off from human feeling.' We didn't know this man's story. We didn't know how he had become like that. But it was enough to know that there must be a story and an attempt to assuage his pain. That in itself enabled us to feel far more patient with him.

I want to make one more point before we move on to the final stage. Sometimes people choose for this stage someone they don't know at all. They use their current pet peeve politician or irritating TV celebrity, or even a historical figure like Hitler. I wouldn't rule this out completely, and you are free to experiment and learn what works for you, but I wouldn't usually recommend it. Your relationship with some TV star or politician is going to be largely based on fantasy. It is usually best to choose people from your own circle of acquaintances. That is likely to be closer to home in terms of your feelings. The purpose of the meditation isn't just to feel more friendliness and kindness while you are sitting with your eyes closed. Your aim has to be to transform your relationships with the people around you, those you meet in your day to day life. From that point of view, your boss at work is a better person to meditate on than Hitler. (Don't try to tell me they're similar!)

14

equalizing the feeling

The final stage of the meditation begins with calling to mind all four people – yourself, your friend, the neutral person, and the person with whom you have difficulty. You make them real for yourself in whatever way you find works best. I tend to imagine that I am sitting with the person I find difficult in front of me, my friend on one side, and the neutral person on the other, so we form a small circle. A circle gives a sense of connectedness and equality which makes it easier to balance the feeling.

I often notice a subtle shift in my energy at this point. I might begin by focusing on each of the four of us in turn, to see where the feeling is strongest, but after a while the loving-kindness becomes a kind of ring of energy that envelops or encloses all four of us. That circle or ring of energy can then expand outwards as this stage develops.

Sometimes people feel uncertain about this part of the meditation, as if they are being asked to impose a kind of bland uniformity on their feelings. But equalizing the feeling of loving-kindness has nothing to do with indifference or tidy emotional accounting. It is about seeing through the more superficial differences of personality and circumstance to the fundamental humanity shared by all four of us.

This beginning section of the fifth stage is described as the development of equanimity. Personally, I have never found the idea of equanimity very exciting. I can respond strongly to becoming more loving, kinder, or wiser, but the thought of being more equanimous just doesn't move me. So I have to unpack it for myself, and see what is involved.

First, I have to peel back from equanimity associations with its near enemies: indifference and a kind of emotional coldness. Equanimity isn't uncaring; it is about having strong feelings for several people equally. As a child at family Christmas celebrations, if I or one of my brothers had asked for and received a 'bigger' present, the others would all be given something, even cash, so that we all got the same value. I never felt my parents were cold or calculating in doing this. It came from love for all their three sons, and their desire to demonstrate that none of us was more or less special.

Equanimity is related to a sense of natural justice. On a societal level, it relates to the desire to see that no one is above the law, that there are no second-class citizens, that all members of society are cared for and protected. Of course, societies never measure up to their ideals, but at the heart of many of them lies the aspiration that everyone should be free to develop their potential, and be helped by the state to avoid sufferings such as starvation or untreated illness. Societies do not measure up to their ideals because their members consistently fail to act in accordance with them, falling back on greed and self-interest, and failing to empathize with others' suffering. While legislation and other ways of changing social conditions can help prevent some manifestations of this, the only real solution is for each of us to do the work on our own hearts, for us to mature as people so that we grow beyond petty self-interest and take other people's suffering to heart. This meditation is a way in which we can school ourselves to do this.

In the charmed circle of your imagination, you work to create an ideal society in miniature, in which the four people symbolize all manner of human beings. In your meditation, at least, they all receive equal care and you aspire for them to realize their potential as human beings. This is despite the fact that some are easy to care about, some leave you cold, and some you find unpleasant, unapproachable, or worse. Holding them in your heart in this way, feeling their value as human beings, you develop an equally strong feeling of friendliness and well-wishing for all of them (not forgetting yourself). With time, this quiet, subtle work in meditation will spill over into how you live your life, and how you treat everyone you meet.

Equanimity isn't just about how you treat other people; it also gives you a great inner freedom. Naturally, we all have our likes and dislikes, and as mild personal preferences, they're fine. What we don't often see is how unhappy they make us when we treat them more seriously. In capitalist societies, we are often encouraged to fine-tune our likes and dislikes in the name of consumer choice. We almost define ourselves by our lifestyle choices. But through doing this more and more, we paint ourselves into a corner. Rather than being open to life, rejoicing in all our experience, we are constantly narrowing down our range of enjoyment. For instance, I live in an English city in which you can buy tea in any food store. But I have developed a taste for almond tea – a black tea with almond flavouring that is available only from one stall in the market square. I no longer enjoy the usual cup of tea at all. So my happiness, regarding tea at least, is dependent on this one source of satisfaction.

It can easily become the same with people. You may have such strong fixed likes and dislikes that you only really feel comfortable under very particular conditions. You may be happy only among people of your own age group, people who share your interest in a particular pastime, people of your own social standing, and so on. Then within that group there may be only a handful of people whose personalities gel with yours. Before you know it, out of all the billions of people on the planet, you're down to half a dozen that you feel really comfortable with. And this constant movement, being pulled towards people you like and pushed to avoid those you dislike, can go on all the time, giving your heart no rest. So likes and dislikes that are natural enough in themselves can end up limiting your freedom of action, and leading you by the nose so that you are never really happy.

Equanimity is the alternative to this. Rather than running a kind of internal check on each person you meet to see whether they have favoured status, whether they're your kind of person and safe to be let into your heart, you could just take away the border guards and the barbed wire and open the frontier of your heart to all comers. Obviously, you don't do this naively; some people *are* untrustworthy and dangerous. But in principle you let everyone in to the extent that it makes sense to do so. You might still have emotional preferences, but you don't let them rule your thoughts and actions.

If you want to get a sense of why this would be a good idea, imagine being with three good friends whom you like so much that you don't mind which one you sit with, or which one you go for a walk with. Now think about being with a good friend, someone you aren't interested in, and someone you dislike. Imagine all the emotional contortions you would go through in order to try to spend time with your friend and not be left struggling to make conversation with the person you don't find interesting, or caught in uneasy proximity to the person you don't like. Even if you are socially adept and could manage to carry this off, it would still cost you a fair amount of effort. Equanimity takes you out of that whole arena, and gives you a serenity that comes from being open to all human beings.

15

all living beings

We must love one another or die.
W. H. Auden

At the beginning of the final stage, we created an imaginary ring of four people including ourselves, and then turned it into a circle of loving-kindness. The rest of the final stage consists of widening out that circle to include limitless numbers of beings. We don't have to take this idea of a circle literally. We aren't trying to keep nice radii of equal length. The geometry of the heart is more organic than that, and has many different possibilities. As we shall see in a minute, there are different ways to go about expanding the loving-kindness to all life.

But first let's address some of the doubts and difficulties that you might have about doing this.

I sometimes have trouble feeling much even for my close friends when practising this meditation. Isn't it a bit unrealistic to expect to produce love for billions of people? There are no expectations. In each meditation, you gently work to set up the conditions for loving feelings to arise. However, as we saw earlier when discussing natural goodness, you do often produce feelings of loving-kindness for thousands of people you have never met. If you hear about innocent people dying in a natural disaster or a terrorist attack, your heart goes out to them. Yes, sure, you may be too tired or too busy to really take in the news. But given the right conditions, you feel for human beings like you who have been drowned, killed in a plane crash, or wounded by a bomb blast. You don't have to force this; it's a natural response of your heart to suffering. You can trust it.

So in this stage you look for this natural response and then nurture it. One way to nurture it is by enjoying it. Caring about other beings, as long as you don't do it in an anxious way, feels enjoyable. There is a sense of rightness and appropriateness about it, as if something deep down within you senses your interconnectedness with all life. When you feel this universal kindness and well-wishing, you have a sense of being in the right relation to the universe.

These things are difficult to talk about, and can easily be misunderstood, or even parodied, which leads me on to the next objection or difficulty that people sometimes raise when they start to work with this final stage.

This generation of universal 'lurve' sounds a bit sentimental and spaced out. Of course, sending love to all life can be done in unhelpful ways. We've seen that every aspect of the practice has its near enemies.

You *can* become sentimental in this last stage, though it isn't the end of the world if you do. The main thing is that, in quite a simple way, you allow your feeling of well-wishing to spread out, putting no limit on it at all.

You are more likely to become a bit spaced out if you treat the meditation as some kind of geography test. For instance, someone in the UK might send love to all the people in Australia, thinking something like, 'Well, there's Sydney (mental picture of the Harbour Bridge), Melbourne (picture a map of southern Australia with vaguely placed dot representing Melbourne), then there's ... what's that place up the top? Is it named after an explorer? Stanley? No, Darwin! And then there's all that space in the middle.' (Mental picture of kangaroos and camels – they read somewhere that there are half a million camels in the Australian outback.) etc. etc.

Of course, it's good to use your imagination. If you have been somewhere, or know something about a place, then by all means use that knowledge to help make it more vivid. But the main aim of seeing these places in your mind's eye is to develop kindness and well-wishing for the people who live there. If you forget to do that, you might as well be doing a general knowledge quiz.

It can really help if you picture people in different parts of the world. If you have friends or relations somewhere, then start by calling them to mind and wishing them well. Then imagine the people around them, and widen the feeling out from there. It is OK to use imagination. I've never been to Africa, so my mental picture of places like Zambia or Chad is very vague, but still I call to mind the people there. Even if I imagine them wearing the wrong kind of clothes and in the wrong landscape with the wrong sounds and smells, still that inaccurate mental picture serves as a link; it enables me to open my heart more than I otherwise would.

I get overwhelmed by the suffering in the world. First, you should congratulate yourself for being open-hearted enough to let in that suffering in the first place. Sometimes it can feel heartbreaking to contemplate the state of the world, and the suffering within it. Turning towards that feeling, even though it can at times feel overwhelming, leads to a very deep place in ourselves. Opening to suffering – rather than running away from it as we so often do – will eventually crack open the hard shell of separate selfhood that keeps us feeling isolated and cut off from life.

In the meantime, if you feel overwhelmed, it is a sign that you need to focus your attention differently. I can best explain this by using the idea that we all have a sphere of concern (things and people we care about) and a sphere of influence (one in which we can act and have an impact). For most of us, the former is by far the bigger. In this heart meditation, our sphere of concern becomes vast; we care for and wish all living beings well. When bad things happen in our sphere of concern – a terrorist atrocity, a child's murder – we can easily feel overwhelmed. We focus on the suffering and feel powerless. But there are two helpful ways in which we can respond. One is by directing loving-kindness to all those involved, the other is to use the incident to motivate us to act positively within our sphere of influence. For example, every act of violence I hear about on the news can motivate me to work harder at writing this book on loving-kindness.

ways to expand the feeling
How do you widen out the feeling of loving-kindness? There are several possibilities. Here are a few suggestions.

geographically
You begin with the circle of care and kindness that surrounds you, your good friend, the neutral person, and the person with whom you have difficulties. It might be just a feeling, or you might see it like a ring of fire, burning with care and love. Or it could be a ring of light. You then allow it to expand in every direction. As in the guided meditation in Chapter 3, first include any other people in the room where you are meditating. (If they are doing the same meditation, it can be a strong experience, knowing that everyone in the room is sending love to each other.) Then you widen out further and further – to everyone in your neighbourhood, your district, perhaps the city in which you live, your country, your continent, all the continents one at a time, then the whole world, until you have included all human beings. (OK, yes, there might be some people in orbit around the Earth. We'll come to them in a minute.)

You needn't stop with human beings. You can include all living beings on this planet: in the oceans, lakes, and rivers; in the air; on land and in the earth. Wish them all well, regardless of whether you like them (horses, cats, dogs, pandas, elephants maybe?), feel neutral towards them (sloths, plankton) or dislike them (flies, snakes, tarantulas, scorpions, Tasmanian devils). They are all part of the community of life sharing this planet.

Then you can open your heart still further, out to wherever you can imagine there may be life. You can send love out beyond the planet (which is where those people on a space station get included). You can imagine life on planets in other galaxies, or even in parallel universes, if you believe they exist. You can also send love to those to come, for instance to those who will inhabit this planet in future.

using the directions of the compass

This is a traditional method found in the Buddhist texts, in which people are sometimes described as radiating love 'in the ten directions'. You send loving-kindness to people in the east, south, west, and north, the intermediate directions – north-east, etc – and then above and below.

calling to mind representative examples

Some people find it hard to connect emotionally with calling to mind vast numbers of people and animals. An alternative approach is to imagine individuals and see them as representing an area or a kind of being. So, for example, if you had a Chilean friend you could imagine them representing everyone in Chile or South America. An image from TV or the Internet of a wounded child could represent for you all the suffering of war-torn parts of the globe; a tiger might be a symbol for all the wildlife that is being pushed towards extinction.

opposites
Another method is to work with pairs of opposites. You can send love and well-wishing to both the young and the old, the rich and the poor, the healthy and the sick, and so on.

freestyle
Simply let your mind roam, allowing images of people to come to mind. You might find yourself jumping around, from images of friends to those in the latest natural disaster, to media celebrities. Just send love and well-wishing to whoever turns up, and gradually strengthen the sense that you are including all life in your feeling.

Whichever method you use, the aim is to open your heart to as many people, as much of life, as you can. There is no need to force it. Just do whatever you can in a particular meditation and trust that it will have an effect. Your heart isn't a tin can, to be somehow prised open. It is a living organism with its times of expansion and contraction. Respect those natural heart movements while doing your best to set up the conditions for it to open as much as possible.

16

views and their effects

All meditation is based on views: what you tell yourself about what you are doing in meditation, what
you are trying to achieve, and how you will get there.
These views provide a kind of foundation on which
the actual practice of meditation is built. How suc-
cessful your meditation will be is partly determined
by the solidity of that foundation of views, so it is
good to examine what you are telling yourself about
the meditation, either consciously or not very
consciously.

We bring to the meditation two kinds of views. First
there are the things that we have been told about it, in
books like this or through a meditation teacher. Then
there are the more general views that we have about
ourselves and about life, taken in ever since we were
very young, which will affect our meditation. Some of
these latter views may run completely contrary to the
meditation itself, and more or less prevent it working.
For instance, you can be working at developing
loving-kindness for yourself, while deep down you

may have a view that you are unlovable or undeserving of love and care. Or you can be working in the meditation to open your heart to other people, while deep down the voice of some adult from your childhood may be whispering to you that opening up and trusting other people only leads to hurt and betrayal. It is very good to try to notice these undermining views, see them as clearly as possible, and do your best to let them go.

two approaches to the meditation
For this meditation there are two basic views: ways in which to explain what you are trying to achieve through the practice and how you can set about it.

1. Seeing the meditation as the conscious development of the qualities of friendliness and love. According to this approach, we currently have a limited capacity for loving-kindness which we can increase through the meditation. In the practice, we find a positive heart-response, perhaps quite weak, and by focusing on it and putting energy into it, we encourage it to grow. It is like lighting a fire. You work to get a small flame going, and then you steadily fan it. If you keep going, and set up the right conditions, from one tiny spark or flame you can eventually produce a conflagration.

2. Seeing the meditation as the conscious unfolding of qualities which are inherent in our heart, but which are usually difficult to access very strongly. According to this view, the practice is about trusting that we are kind and loving in our deepest nature, and clearing the obstacles that stand in the way of experiencing and expressing that. Rather than fanning a flame, the image here would be more like cleaning a grimy window to allow the sun to shine through.

Either of these ways of approaching the meditation can be effective, and you may even find it helpful to use both at different times. The developmental approach is perhaps closer to our everyday experience. When we sit to meditate, we often do not immediately feel much love or generosity towards other people, but by focusing on whatever positive feelings are there, and feeding them with phrases, ideas, and imagination, the feelings do grow in the course of the practice. We can have a sense that if we keep nurturing these feelings over a long period of time, we can gradually transform ourself into someone very kind, generous, and loving.

The unfoldment approach is very encouraging, particularly if we are lacking in self-esteem. Far from being poor and useless, according to many great Buddhist teachers human beings are inherently loving and compassionate, but we have lost touch with that deeper level of ourselves. By tuning in to our heart's deep feelings and purifying ourselves of superficial negativities, we can tap into a radiance of love and generosity that is as natural as breathing.

While both views have their advantages, either can tend to an unhelpful extreme if you take them in the wrong way. One of the arts of meditation is learning to make the appropriate amount of effort. Following the developmental approach may tend to encourage a kind of forced or willed effort ('I'm going to get this fire going if it kills me!'), and a lack of trust in yourself and the meditation. Following the unfoldment approach, you may be more relaxed, but you might not make sufficient effort ('I know the sun's there, so I'll clean this window another day.') At the extremes, the developmental view leads to a crude, huffing and puffing kind of meditation; the unfoldment view tends to daydreaming and wool-gathering.

I used to teach very much from the developmental point of view, but these days I operate more from the unfoldment approach – while still emphasizing the need for a gentle, steady effort in meditation – as I find it is more encouraging for people.

One approach may seem more natural to you than the other. If that is the case, then you should follow that. If you feel drawn to both, then I suggest you adopt the stance that you can trust in your deep heart feeling, but that you still need to make the effort in meditation to allow that feeling to shine through.

interconnectedness

One of the most common questions I get asked about this meditation is 'Does it literally affect other people?' This is a very important issue. If you believe that by taking the time to meditate you are not just affecting yourself but actually having an effect on others, even making a contribution to world peace, then you have another powerful motivation to make the effort to sit down and do it. So what is your view? Can our thoughts and feelings affect the world around us?

Our mental states certainly seem to have an impact on those around us. Even animals pick up on it. There are Buddhist monks living in jungle areas in Thailand and Sri Lanka who regularly encounter tigers, bears, and other dangerous animals, and who claim that by radiating loving-kindness towards the animals, they remain unharmed. The Buddha himself is said to have stopped a wild elephant from attacking him through directing loving thoughts towards it.

But does sending love to people on the other side of the planet have any effect? Personally, I have no doubt that loving-kindness has a subtle but definite influence on those to whom it is directed, though the western scientific jury is still out on this question. Our views of what is possible are often based on old Newtonian assumptions about the world. But quantum physics suggests that the world is far stranger, more magical, and more interconnected than we had previously believed. In moving into a strange world where time and space are no longer what we had assumed, western science is occupying ground that has been familiar territory to advanced Buddhist meditators for the last 2,500 years.

what happens after death

In practising this meditation, we may sooner or later be brought up against another fundamental view: our idea of what happens after death. Another of my FAQs from new (and not so new) meditators is 'Can I use this meditation to send love to someone who has died?'

Here, western science with its materialist assumptions will tend to answer no, or perhaps more gently, 'You can do it if you find it comforting psychologically, but consciousness ceases at death so there is no deceased person to receive your love.'

After all, what experiment could you design, what data could you use, to verify any other opinion? But according to Buddhist tradition, death is not annihilation. The stream of consciousness continues. This is how, for example, the Dalai Lama comes to be considered the latest in a long line of teachers. So by all means send love to those you know who have died. Many people who have lost someone close to them feel quite powerless in the face of their loss. Sending loving-kindness to a relative or friend who has died is empowering for you, and may well have a very positive influence on the consciousness of the deceased person.

17

the meditation and everyday life

practising during the day

Although meditation can be enjoyable in itself, the purpose of practising is to change your life. You want the effects of focusing on your heart in meditation to overflow so that you are more open-hearted, more emotionally buoyant, as you go through the day. In my experience of watching many hundreds of people doing this meditation, they do in time become friendlier, kinder, more patient, and more loving. I can think of quite a few people whose spouses (who didn't meditate themselves) actively encouraged them to keep practising because they had discovered that loving-kindness meditation made them much easier to live with!

Sometimes you might sit to meditate and feel that nothing much is happening. You do your best to contact your feelings, to empathize with others, and to wish yourself and others well, but it all feels rather grey and flat. You get up feeling that the meditation has been a waste of time. But then, hours later, you are suddenly hit by a wave of kindness for yourself, or when talking to someone, you are caught by an unexpected sense of care and concern for them. There was a delayed effect from the practice. I know people who have faithfully meditated for months or even years, and feeling that nothing much was happening during the meditation itself. But they kept going because they noticed positive changes in themselves outside of meditation. So there is a dialogue between your meditation practice and your experience during the rest of the day. As you keep practising, it will become clearer that meditation is positively affecting your mental states in other areas of life.

Although the meditation will have an effect in itself, you can speed up the process of emotional transformation by taking time during the day to focus on your heart and to wish yourself and others well. It may be as little as a moment or two, or you could find several minutes in which to do a short loving-kindness meditation. Here are some examples of ways of practising during the day that I find helpful.

> On first waking up in the morning, before getting out of bed, take a few moments to wish yourself well and that your day may be fulfilling, enjoyable, and productive. Call to mind all the millions of people who are also starting a new day – some with excitement, some with anxiety, some feeling spacious and expansive, some hoping somehow to get through it. There are even some who will not live to see the end of it. Just

take a few seconds to open your heart to them as well, these other human beings like you. You can do the same before you go to sleep, wishing yourself and all beings a good night's rest and happy dreams.

Before going into a meeting, or going to see someone, call to mind those you will be meeting with, allow yourself to empathize with them, and wish them well. Even if you have never met the person before, and only have their name as a kind of link, it is still useful to send them loving-kindness. I find that the meeting somehow tends to go better when I have done this preliminary work on myself. You can briefly do the same thing before making a call or composing an email.

Use 'dead' time – in a traffic jam, waiting for a bus or train, in the departure lounge, waiting for your computer to boot up, and so on – to do a mini-meditation on loving-kindness. With practice, rather than being times when you become impatient, or just 'dull out' and become unaware, these periods of waiting can become rich and enjoyable. Rather than being at the mercy of the external situation, you are using the time for something that will benefit you and others.

Whenever you hear news that someone is ill, in trouble, has had an accident, or suffered any kind of misfortune, just take a few moments to wish them well.

Through using opportunities like these to practise open-heartedness during the day, you will reinforce your formal meditation. You will find your meditation practice will go more easily, and positive change will come about more quickly.

Through a combination of formal meditation and daily life practice you will be able over time to bring about radical changes in yourself. In the words of Trungpa Rinpoche, a famous Tibetan lama who taught in both the UK and the USA, you will 'stop being a nuisance to life'. Instead, you will increasingly become a benign influence in all the situations that life brings you.

ethics

Over time, the meditation will make you aware of the ways in which how you live supports open-heartedness and those things that work against it. The latter can feel very uncomfortable. For a while you may feel torn between some favourite old habits and a growing sense that they are not supporting your efforts at loving-kindness. As your heart opens, you are likely to find yourself more sensitive to ethical issues. This may be inconvenient, but if your heart has really started to open, there is nothing for it but to look these issues in the eye. A couple of areas in which this can arise are attitudes to eating meat and to ecology.

vegetarianism

As you keep on practising this meditation, wishing well to all living beings in the final stage, you might start to feel uneasy about having some of them killed on your behalf so that you can eat them. Admittedly, not all Buddhists are vegetarian, though in some cases this is because they live in a harsh environment in which it is hard to grow vegetables. There are also some people whose health suffers if they avoid animal products completely. However, most of us can live very well and healthily without eating animals, and I found that when I became a vegetarian after learning this meditation, I felt on better terms with myself and the world.

There are complex issues here, as even eating eggs or using milk products still involves a great deal of animal suffering. There is a whole spectrum between total violence and absolute non-violence. No one manages to be at either extreme. All we can do is be honest with ourselves about where we stand within that spectrum and do what we can to move in the direction of greater compassion.

cradling the world

These days it is clearer than ever before how interconnected we are, not just with other human beings, but with all life. The effects of our lifestyle on the environment are more dramatic (and in many ways scarier) than ever before. So another area into which this meditation naturally leads is ecological awareness, concern for this planet on which we live and on which future generations of beings will live (if we are not extinct by then).

Sooner or later, loving-kindness meditation brings us up against the way in which we feel that we are the centre of things. As we move through the stages of the meditation, we become aware that all other living beings also hold themselves dear, feel themselves to be a centre of life, in just the same way. In this way, we see that, though we ourselves are unique and valuable, we aren't any more unique and valuable than other living beings. We also become aware how interconnected we are with all life. As we've seen, just to drink a cup of tea or coffee involves a great network stretching across the planet.

This interconnectedness is the first principle of 'deep ecology',[6] whose proponents believe that having such an anthropocentric (human-centred) view of life goes against the reality of the web of interrelated and interacting life. Instead of seeing human beings as unique and special, this theory argues for the adoption of a more ecocentric attitude. If we and the planet are to survive, we need to have a less dominating and proprietorial approach, and see ourselves as part of the fabric of life.

The second principle of deep ecology is the need for human self-realization. Instead of identifying with our egos or those near and dear to us, we would learn to identify with all life, the whole ecosphere. This would require a radical change of consciousness, but it would bring our behaviour into line with what scientists are saying is necessary for the well-being of life on Earth. It is this radical change of consciousness that we get some glimpse of in the last stage of loving-kindness meditation. When that stage goes well, your heart is open to all life, and you feel much more identified with it. If you could live out of that state all the time, you would not deliberately do things that you know damage the planet any more than you would deliberately harm your own body.

Through looking at issues such as this, and through observation of your own experience, you arrive at a natural ethical sense. This natural ethic isn't about 'thou shalt nots' or sanctions. It arises directly from seeing the suffering you cause to others, and experience yourself, when your heart is closed.

In particular, you will find yourself becoming more sensitive to the suffering of living beings – both human and animal. This natural ethical sense, based on love and open-heartedness, expresses itself through a life that is as harmless and non-violent as possible. That doesn't mean being weak or ineffectual: think of Gandhi, whose non-violence helped to change the lives of millions of people. You can still stand up for what you believe to be right; you can still oppose injustice and tyranny. You just become increasingly wary of using force in order to do so.

This doesn't mean that at times force might not be necessary, but it becomes a last resort, used with regret and still within a context of concern and kind feeling. For instance, if a mad axe-man ran amok in my local supermarket, I would take the opportunity to sneak up behind him and knock him out with a frozen baguette. We live in a very imperfect world, and there are always hard decisions to make about relative degrees of harm. But I would do it feeling compassion for someone who was mad enough to wield an axe among the shopping aisles, and I wouldn't hit him any harder than was absolutely necessary.

18

difficulties on the way

What is it like to practise this meditation over months and years? Are there stages you go through, and where do you end up with it? Although this book is aimed mainly at beginners, it is good to have an overview of how your practice may develop. It can inspire you and, when the unexpected happens, also give you a sense that this is all part of the practice. We shall start by looking at a few difficulties that might crop up – though they are all really the 'growing pains' of the practice. Then in the next chapter we'll look at how the meditation can flower.

the heart as unknown territory – discovering uncomfortable feelings
A few years ago, a keeper at a zoo in the west of England found himself facing a stampede of people. They were all running in panic away from one of the enclosures. When he asked what was going on, they yelled back, 'The wallaby has escaped!'

On a visit to Australia years ago, a friend took me to Melbourne Zoo. At one point, we walked through a

grassy area, along with other visitors including parents with young children in pushchairs. There were a
number of wallabies, all tamely hopping about. Wallabies don't pose any threat to humans, but those
English zoo visitors didn't realize that. To them, a
wallaby was a strange animal from the other side of
the world. Who knew what havoc it might cause? So
they ran for their lives.

I am often reminded of this story when I watch
people exploring their emotions through meditation.
As time goes on, they begin to find emotional responses emerging that they didn't know were there.
At that point, their first response is often to do the internal equivalent of bolting, and yelling, 'The wallaby
has escaped!' The unknown is always a bit scary, but
it is usually our nervous or fearful response to it that
causes the problem, rather than the emotion itself.
Once you get used to this new feeling, it generally
turns out to be something that enriches your emotional life, another colour on the palette of your
feelings.

What makes things difficult is that we often first
experience feelings after they have been repressed
for a long time. As we practise emotional awareness
and honesty, we start to discover that there are some
aspects of ourselves that we have not wanted to look
at, or that we might have denied completely. As we
start turning towards them, they respond like people
or animals that have been kept under lock and key,
angry or depressed from having been locked up. Or,
while we are still making up our minds about

whether to let them out, they make a sudden bolt for freedom which startles or scares us.

Rather than thinking better of it and closing the door again, we need to see that it isn't these repressed aspects of ourselves that are the problem. We have made them problematic by hiding them away out of sight. Given their freedom, and allowed to bask in the sunshine of our awareness for a while, they will soon be grazing peacefully.

Some people seem naturally quite equable and easy-going. When I introduce them to the five-stage loving-kindness meditation, these people often say they cannot think of anybody to put in the fourth stage of the practice. There is no one they really dislike or have difficulties with. But after meditating for a few months, the picture changes. They start complaining that they are finding themselves more irritable and bad-tempered. Whereas to start with they couldn't find any candidates for the fourth stage, they now have a queue of people waiting to be put into it. Understandably, these meditators feel that something is going badly wrong.

I don't see it like that. It is hard to see how working to develop loving-kindness could really make you grouchier and shorten your fuse. What has happened is that the meditation is making these people aware of feelings that were present all along. Like many people, when I started to meditate I wasn't really in touch with my heart. In fact I wasn't very aware of my feelings at all. Meditating on loving-kindness brought me closer to what was happening. My feelings changed from monochrome to living colour, and I began to notice all kinds of emotional responses and reactions that I had not seen before. Some of them were pleasant discoveries: bursts of happiness, out-breaks of generous feeling, and so on. But some of them were a bit of a shock. Having thought of myself as generally quite good-natured and on good terms with the world, I was forced to admit that I was some-times irritable, tetchy, unkind, and uncaring.

Recognizing these less desirable feelings was diffi-cult, but I eventually came to appreciate the value of my discovery. After all, although I liked my picture of myself as benign and caring, if it wasn't completely true there was no point in having a self-image that didn't fit the reality. Most of our suffering in life stems from the fact that our idea of how things are (or ought to be) doesn't square with how life actually is. So although I didn't like it, I knew I was better off with a more complex, and truer, self-image. And ob-viously if there were things going on in my emotional life that were happening below the radar of self-awareness, there was nothing I could do about them. If I didn't recognize my irritation with someone at work, it would spill out in ways that I hadn't in-tended, such as jokes at their expense, and subtle put-downs. What you don't know about you have no power to change. Finally, I had to admit that I felt more alive when I was vividly in touch with my emo-tions, in all their mixed glory. Although I didn't like feeling angry, miserable, and so on, it was all better than feeling a bland nothingness.

Many people manage to be patient with others but fail to be patient with themselves. This is often because they expect too much of themselves. I remember many years ago leading a Buddhism course for beginners. By the third week there was an odd atmosphere, and I tried to work out what was going on. I eventually realized that most of the people in the group did not feel good about themselves – they felt they should be better than they were – then along came Vessantara and started talking about love, wisdom, and compassion. This increased their expectations of themselves even more, and their sense of failing to live up to them was intensified. So I had to try another tack to sort things out.

It is very easy to fail to live up to your own expectations and to be constantly critical of your own efforts. When you practise meditation, it is OK to expect things of yourself, but you also need to be very patient and understanding as well. After all, radically changing your responses to life is perhaps the most difficult thing you could ever do as a human being. To transform yourself into an embodiment of open-hearted friendliness, you really need to be sympathetic to yourself.

dragons guarding the treasure
In many myths and stories, a great treasure is guarded by something you really wouldn't want to have to face, perhaps a dragon or a giant. This is also true of meditation. People sometimes give up just at the point when they are getting close to some real inner treasure, because they have an unpleasant

experience and assume they must be off-track. Let's look at a couple of examples.

The first dragon guarding the treasure of inner happiness is often boredom. As we turn inward in meditation, we leave behind outer stimuli. We are no longer watching TV, listening to music, chatting to friends, making love, or drinking coffee. There is just our own mind, our own heart. This can be an awkward transition. Nothing exciting is happening. For a mind that has been used to a great deal of stimulation, it can feel as if there is a big empty space. At this point, the natural tendency is to fill that space with something. Deprived of external interest, we use our mind as a home cinema to keep us entertained. Rather than be bored, we lose ourselves in ideas, memories, even worries and anxieties – anything rather than face that empty space.

At this point, it really helps if you remember the 'dragon guarding the treasure' teaching. Boredom is a sign that you are moving from being caught up in thoughts towards inner stillness. It feels like a kind of desert that you have to cross as you travel from one to the other. But it is not really a wasteland. It only appears that way because you are not taking enough interest in your present experience. The secret at this point is to allow yourself to become curious about this experience that we label boredom. What is it really like? If you stay with what is happening, rather than running away and going to look for more stimulus, the desert will blossom.

The second dragon is sadness. As a result of practising this meditation, our hearts start to open more fully and more often. When this happens, the first thing we experience is often the sadness of having kept our heart closed. For some people, that sadness can be very strong, a deep pain. It is natural to try to avoid it, but avoiding your experience leads to a kind of deadness that is worse than pain and sadness. If you stay with it, the dragon will give you its treasure. Part of staying with it may involve forgiving yourself for having kept your heart closed for so long, and for all the hurt you might have caused as a result.

long-term issues

Meditation is gradual magic. Through meditation we can transform ourselves in very deep ways, but it isn't usually a quick fix. As you keep practising, you may find certain issues coming up again and again. It may be a difficult relationship with a family member, a deep-seated attitude you have, or an old sadness that is haunting you. This is only to be expected. Meditation increases awareness and brings things to the surface.

With experience, you learn to sit patiently with these things, turning towards them with kindness. These are the stuff of your humanity, and as you learn, often slowly and painfully, to hold them in awareness with a welcoming attitude, they gradually transform. You learn to trust that issues that keep presenting themselves are doing so in order to be healed.

If I go away to practise meditation intensively, I can guarantee that at some point I shall revisit all the most painful parts of my life: the deaths of my parents and other dark times. However, although these things still turn up, they no longer have the emotional charge they used to. They are more like old friends with whom I have shared hard times. The pain has largely gone.

the impossible thing

Sooner or later, you are likely to come up against the Impossible Thing – something you feel you will never be able to change. It usually feels like something completely unacceptable, that makes you unlovable as a person, and unworthy of others' kindness and generosity. It is the reason why you keep away from people, and why you run away from intimacy. If people found out about it, they would reject you forever. But probably before they had a chance to act, you would just die on the spot, of shame, fear, and embarrassment. (You may also avoid getting close to other people in order to protect them from the Impossible Thing.) So you are stuck. You curse your fate. You see other people struggling with aspects of themselves, but those don't seem so bad. You know that you could work with the issues and tendencies that they find difficult about themselves. It is you who have been cursed with the one thing that is impossible to face or deal with. What are you to do? Burdened with the Impossible Thing, you will never get anywhere with meditation or Buddhism. Others will cross the finishing line of life with the shining faces and clenched fists of dreams achieved. You're going to have to skulk off into the bushes and disappear.

As usual, the solution – and there *is* one, though it will take time – is to turn towards your experience. Through patient, kindly awareness, you can learn to accept the unacceptable. It is your resistance to it that gives the Impossible Thing its strength and energy. The more you engage with it, hopeless as that seems at first, the more possibility there is of it being trans-formed. Eventually, dealing with the Impossible Thing stops feeling like Mission Impossible and be-comes just another aspect of the work you are doing in meditation.

You may even get to the stage where you take the great risk of comparing your experience in this area with that of other people. If you and they are very open with one another, you will discover that you are not special in this regard. Others also have their Impossible Thing. If they knew about yours, they wouldn't think it was so bad. From their point of view, what *they* have to face is truly unworkable. This can help put your personal *bête noire* into perspective. It may also help you to see that beneath our social façades we human beings are eccentric, weird, and wonderful. We are busy trying to live up to one another's expectations of what is normal, when we are all a mixture of the sublime and the ridiculous. How we are in ourselves is actually more interesting, and more lovable, than the watered-down and well-scripted ways in which we usually try to present our-selves to one another.

19

the flowering of loving-kindness

Meditation is concerned fundamentally with the present. When you are meditating on loving-kindness, you need to be aware of your experience in the present moment and to keep turning towards it with a kindly awareness. But to inspire yourself and stay motivated to carry out the day-to-day work of meditation, it can be very useful to look ahead and see where your practice can lead in the long-term. In the previous chapter, we looked at some of the difficulties on the path of meditation; in this final one, we'll look briefly at some of the joys and benefits. But we'll start with some practical steps you can take in order to take the meditation further.

where do I go from here?
The bottom line is: keep practising! As with most things, regular practice – even for a few minutes – is more effective than meditating for an hour one day and then doing nothing for ten days. However, do

what you can. Any steps you take in the direction of becoming more kind and open-hearted will be satisfying for you and will benefit others as well. The world needs all the loving-kindness that any of us can muster.

If you want to take things further, it would be helpful to learn more about meditation and Buddhism. A good starting point is to read a little more about loving-kindness meditation. You will find some suggestions in the Resources section. However, meditation is an individual matter and no book can give you all the guidance you need. There is no substitute for having a teacher.

There are many Buddhist centres and meditation teachers around these days. Don't expect the person who teaches your local meditation class to be highly enlightened, but they should have been practising meditation for several years and have been authorized to teach. In making contact with a teacher in this way, you will also make a link to a *sangha* – a community of practitioners who are involved with that centre or teacher. Whether or not you like joining groups, contact with other people who, like you, are meditating and working to transform themselves can be very supportive.

the immeasurables

So where does practising this meditation lead? Loving-kindness can go on developing indefinitely. There may be a limit to how many people you can call to mind at one time, but your heart never runs out of storage space. When it fully opens, it can contain the whole of life. For this reason, loving-kindness is described as 'immeasurable' in some Buddhist texts. It appears as part of a set of feelings known as the 'four immeasurables'.[7] The other three are compassion, joy in others' happiness, and equanimity. Loving-kindness, friendliness, an openness to life, is the basic positive feeling, but it can widen out and take on these different emotional flavours. When it comes into contact with someone who is suffering, it changes into compassion. When it meets with someone who is happy, it transforms into delight in their happiness. When it is developed without any partiality, it becomes equanimity.

There are specific methods of meditation for developing each of these immeasurables, but they are beyond the scope of this book. In any case, if you practise this meditation for developing loving-kindness, you will find the other immeasurables appearing naturally. For instance, in the second stage, if you call to mind a friend who has recently had some good news and wish them well, you naturally rejoice in their happiness and good fortune. Or in the third stage, if you become aware of the suffering in the life of your neutral person, you will feel compassion towards them, out of empathy, knowing that, like you, they long not to suffer.

the meditation and insight into the nature of things
This loving-kindness meditation is very highly valued in the Buddhist tradition. However, the view of the traditional texts is that it will not take you all the way to direct intuitive experience of the true nature

of things – which is the central goal of Buddhism. They say that meditation on loving-kindness will 'only' take you into concentrated, refined, and blissful states of mind! There are some Buddhist teachers who disagree with this. Even if it is true, there is no doubt that this meditation takes you to a point from which it is relatively easy to take that final leap into the heart of reality.

If the meditation goes *really* well, then by the final stage you are like a great beacon of love, ablaze with the fire of well-wishing for all living beings. To use a traditional image, you care for them all, longing for their happiness, as if you were a mother and each of them was your only child. You feel incredibly close to each and every one of them. At this point, you are very near to a direct experience of how things really are. You just need to let go of thinking in terms of a 'self' that feels love for 'others'. Then suddenly the whole subject–object duality will fall apart. You will emerge into an indescribable world in which there is no separation, and it is as natural to care about another person as it is to care about your own hand. There will be no 'me' standing apart from 'others'. There will just be love.

You may also find that your loving-kindness opens out into a kind of formless meditation, in which you no longer focus on anything or anyone in particular. It is as if you go beyond making any conceptual distinction between living beings and the rest of your experience. You throw open the doors of your heart to all life, to the whole of your experience – whatever it is – as it flows moment by moment through that heart space.

the fulfilled heart –
awakening great compassion

With insight into the nature of things, it dawns on you that your picture of the world – me and them, mine and yours, etc. – is just a useful description of life, not how things actually are. At that point, two things happen. First you become aware of the tremendous aliveness, freedom, and energy of the heart, which has been overlaid and stifled by all your misguided judging and conceptualizing. You get a glimpse of what is possible, the tremendously inspiring prospect of total freedom. However, at the same time, your open heart feels very intensely the suffering with which it is surrounded: from a toddler crying for its parents to refugees fleeing from torture and oppression. More than that, you see that a great deal of this suffering is, in a sense, unnecessary. It is all brought about by wrong interpretations of the world. Just as we can see that someone who is highly paranoid creates their own suffering, interpreting everyday situations as threatening and dangerous, so an enlightened person can see that we too create much of our suffering by how we interpret our experience.

Someone who has travelled far down the path to Awakening sees a heartbreaking situation. They know that in the depths of the heart of every being lies tremendous joy, love, and freedom. Yet they watch people scurrying in all directions trying to find some external source of happiness to hang on to. It takes a great deal of courage to turn towards this tragic situation with loving awareness, to feel all this suffering directly, to open your heart to it. If you do manage to open yourself in this way, then rather than breaking, your heart opens to its fullest extent. The deepest and most miraculous powers of a human being are drawn out in response, and you awaken the great compassion of a bodhisattva. A bodhisattva is someone whose heart is set on gaining the fullness of human potential, total love and wisdom, so that they can then help others to escape from the suffering in which they are languishing through misunderstanding the nature of their experience.

This is true fulfilment; the bodhisattva is in process of realizing their deepest heart-wish for themselves and others – though they do not see 'self' and 'other' as ultimately separate. They are at the service of wisdom and compassion, enabling them to shine out in the world with ever greater power.

So much of the world's suffering is brought about by human greed and hatred. Wars, terrorist atrocities, human devastation of the environment, and other sources of misery all begin from a movement in someone's heart. They all start from feelings such as insecurity, resentment, and greed, which become rationalized and then objectified in actions. The bomb-destroyed buildings, the devastated rainforests, are all expressions of something deeply wrong in the hearts of the human beings that caused them: a closedness, a lack of connection, a failure of empathy with other living beings. Because all this suffering originates in the heart, it can also be brought to an end by working to open your own heart and helping others to do the same. You may be a very long way from being a bodhisattva, but by practising this meditation with the motivation to benefit yourself and others, rather than being part of the problem, you are becoming part of the solution (in however small a way) to the world's suffering.

notes

1 This discourse is found twice in the Pali Canon, at *Sutta Nipata* i.8, and at *Khuddakapatha* 9.

2 *Anguttara Nikaya* v.342, commented on in *The Path of Purification (Visuddhimagga)*, a meditation text by the great fifth-century Theravada Buddhist commentator Buddhaghosa. See chapter 9, 59–76.

3 'Awakened heart' is a translation of the Sanskrit term *bodhicitta*.

4 The term in Pali is *metta*, and in Sanskrit *maitri* (pronounced 'my-tree' with the emphasis on the first syllable). So loving-kindness meditation is known in Indian Buddhism as *metta* or *maitri bhavana*: 'development of loving-kindness'.

5 This way of practising in five stages is based on a tradition that is articulated in Buddhaghosa's *The Path of Purification*, chapter 9, 1–58.

6 An environmental movement initiated in the early 1970s by the Norwegian philosopher Arne Naess.

7 The Sanskrit for 'immeasurable' is *apramana*. The 'immeasurables' are also sometimes called the 'four divine abodes' (Pali: *brahma vihara*).

resources

books
Wildmind: A Step-by-Step Guide to Meditation by Bodhipaksa, Windhorse Publications, 2003.
Based on the popular Wildmind meditation teaching website, this book offers a clear and practical approach to meditation, with a section on loving-kindness.

Meditation: The Buddhist Way of Tranquillity and Insight by Kamalashila, Windhorse Publications, 1999.
A useful and systematic introduction to Buddhist meditation, with sections on loving-kindness meditation and the four immeasurables.

Change Your Mind – A Practical Guide to Buddhist Meditation by Paramananda, Windhorse Publications, 1996.
Introduces meditation on the breath and on positive emotion, and then explores intention, balanced effort, and other helpful topics with a poetic lightness.

Lovingkindness – The Revolutionary Art of Happiness by Sharon Salzberg, Shambhala Publications, 2003.
A book about loving-kindness in meditation and in

everyday life, by a well-known American teacher of *vipassana* meditation.

A Heart as Wide as the World: Stories on the Path of Lovingkindness by Sharon Salzberg, Shambhala Publications, 1999.
A follow-up book to *Lovingkindness*, with more practical advice, stories, and reflections.

Living with Kindness: The Buddha's Teaching on Metta by Sangharakshita, Windhorse Publications, 2004.
An exposition of the *Metta Sutta,* the quintessential traditional Buddhist text on loving-kindness.

Buddhism with an Attitude by B. Alan Wallace, Snow Lion Publications, 2003.
One of many books available on *lojong* – a Tibetan system of mind training for developing the qualities of a bodhisattva.

The Breath by Vessantara, Windhorse Publications, 2005.
My book on breath awareness meditation forms a companion to this one. It gives guidance on some fundamental issues about meditation that will also be helpful for loving-kindness meditation.

websites
www.fwbo.org – Here you will find links to Buddhist centres around the world in which loving-kindness meditation is taught in the five-stage format described in this book.

www.vessantara.net – My website, containing articles, meditation materials, my teaching schedule, and details of publications and recordings.

www.wildmind.org – A website offering online meditation courses, including material on heart meditations, as well as guided meditation CDs.

www.ahs.org.uk – The website of Lama Shenpen Hookham. Her very heart-based approach to Buddhism has been an influence on this book.

www.theforgivenessproject.com – Includes inspiring personal accounts from people who chose to respond to violence with loving-kindness and forgiveness.

The windhorse symbolizes the energy of the Enlightened mind carrying the truth of the Buddha's teachings to all corners of the world. On its back the windhorse bears three jewels: a brilliant gold jewel represents the Buddha, the ideal of Enlightenment, a sparkling blue jewel represents the teachings of the Buddha, the Dharma, and a glowing red jewel, the community of the Buddha's enlightened followers, the Sangha. Windhorse Publications, through the medium of books, similarly takes these three jewels out to the world.

Windhorse Publications is a Buddhist publishing house, staffed by practising Buddhists. We place great emphasis on producing books of high quality, accessible and relevant to those interested in Buddhism at whatever level. Drawing on the whole range of the Buddhist tradition, our books include translations of traditional texts, commentaries, books that make links with Western culture and ways of life, biographies of Buddhists, and works on meditation.

As a charitable institution we welcome donations to help us continue our work. We also welcome manuscripts on aspects of Buddhism or meditation. For orders and catalogues log on to www.windhorsepublications.com or contact:

Windhorse Publications	Consortium	Windhorse Books
11 Park Road	1045 Westgate Drive	P O Box 574
Birmingham	St Paul MN 55114	Newtown NSW 2042
B13 8AB	USA	Australia
UK		

Windhorse Publications is an arm of the Friends of the Western Buddhist Order, which has more than sixty centres on four continents. Through these centres, members of the Western Buddhist Order offer regular programmes of events for the general public and for more experienced students. These include meditation classes, public talks, study on Buddhist themes and texts, and bodywork classes such as t'ai chi, yoga, and massage. The FWBO also runs several retreat centres and the Karuna Trust, a fundraising charity that supports social welfare projects in the slums and villages of India.

Many FWBO centres have residential spiritual communities and ethical businesses associated with them. Arts activities are encouraged too, as is the development of strong bonds of friendship between people who share the same ideals. In this way the FWBO is developing a unique approach to Buddhism, not simply as a set of techniques, but as a creatively directed way of life for people living in the modern world.

If you would like more information about the FWBO please visit the website at www.fwbo.org or write to:

London Buddhist Centre	Aryaloka	Sydney Buddhist Centre
51 Roman Road	14 Heartwood Circle	24 Enmore Road
London	Newmarket NH 03857	Sydney NSW 2042
E2 0HU	USA	Australia
UK		

ALSO FROM WINDHORSE PUBLICATIONS

CHANGE YOUR MIND:
A PRACTICAL GUIDE TO BUDDHIST MEDITATION

PARAMANANDA

Buddhism is based on the truth that, with effort, we can change the way we are. But how? Among the many methods Buddhism has to offer, meditation is the most direct. It is the art of getting to know one's own mind and learning to encourage what is best in us.

This bestseller is an approachable and thorough guide to meditation, based on traditional material but written in a light and modern style. Colourfully illustrated with anecdotes and tips from the author's experience as a meditator and teacher, it also offers refreshing inspiration to seasoned meditators.

208 pages, with photographs
ISBN 1 899579 75 3
£9.99/$13.95/€13.95

THE BREATH

VESSANTARA

The breath: always with us, necessary to our very existence, but often unnoticed. Yet giving it attention can transform our lives.

This is a very useful combination of practical instruction on the mindfulness of breathing with much broader lessons on where the breath can lead us. Vessantara, a meditator of many years experience, offers us:

> * Clear instruction on how to meditate on the breath
> * Practical ways to integrate meditation into our lives
> * Suggestions for deepening calm and concentration
> * Advice on how to let go and dive into experience
> * Insights into the lessons of the breath

The Breath returns us again and again to the fundamental and precious experience of being alive.

111 pages
ISBN 1 899579 69 9
£6.99/$10.95/€10.95

*The **art of meditation** series continues with **The Body**, available mid 2007.*

the art of meditation series

Meditation is a skill, a tool, an art. It offers us many ways into peace, happiness, joy, self-knowledge, compassion, and wisdom. There are a multitude of Buddhist meditation practices. While many books try to describe them all together, each book in this series will provide a more intensive look at an individual meditation.

At the core of each book will be a practical introduction to the meditation under consideration. In the case of many of the titles, there will also be reference to a broader applicability of awareness of the breath, the development of positive emotions, and awareness of the body.

There are several levels planned for this series.

The introductory level includes:
- The breath: the mindfulness of breathing
- The heart: loving-kindness
- The body: body scans and walking meditation

Further levels may include:
- The brahma vihāras ('sublime abodes')
- Satipaṭṭhāna or Ānāpānasati
- Pure awareness
- The six element practice
- Visualization

— the art of meditation is the art of life —